THE RHETORIC OF WAR

*Language, Argument, and Policy
During the Vietnam War*

Harvey Averch

University Press of America,® Inc.
Lanham · New York · Oxford

**Copyright © 2002 by
University Press of America,® Inc.**
4720 Boston Way
Lanham, Maryland 20706
UPA Acquisitions Department (301) 459-3366

PO Box 317
Oxford
OX2 9RU, UK

ISBN 0-7618-2421-9 (paperback : alk. ppr.)

For
Barbara, Elizabeth, and Carrie

Think first, before you get into war, about how much of it is beyond calculation. For as it goes on, it tends to end up mostly as a matter of chances that we have equal inability to control, and which way they will turn out is unforeseeable in our hour of danger. When men go to war, they begin by taking action, which they ought to do last, and only after they have suffered do they engage in discussion. Since neither we nor, apparently, you have made such a mistake yet, we tell you, as long as sound deliberation is still a free choice for both of us, do not break the treaty, do not transgress your oaths, but arbitrate our differences in accordance with our agreement. If you do not, we, with the gods we have sworn by as our witnesses, will attempt to defend ourselves against any move you initiate.

— Thucydides, *The Peloponnesian War*. (Lattimore edition, 1998, pp. 38-39)

CONTENTS

PREFACE

I began this policy history of the Vietnam War a long time ago, in 1968, just after the Tet offensive. Except for sampling the emerging historical and strategic literature, I did not renew work on it for 30 years, long after passion in the United States over the war had died, and its longer term outcome was much clearer. Vietnam, the country unified by the North Vietnamese in 1975, has not turned out to be the bitter, permanent, malevolent enemy it was predicted to become but more a "normal" international adversary of the United States.

The United States lost the war. Yet it survived and prospered to become the only economic and military superpower left. When it lost, the dominoes of Southeast Asia that U.S. decisionmakers persistently forecast would fall did not do so. Vietnam itself has become an adherent of state capitalism, doing deals with American manufacturers. The United States occasionally cooperates with this adversary, and sometimes opposes it. The current U.S. ambassador to Hanoi is a former prisoner of war. The then Secretary of Defense, William Cohen, visited Hanoi in summer 2000 followed by President Clinton in the fall.

Revisions to the standard revisionist history of a United States with perverse economic or political intentions in entering the war are now beginning to appear. I try to keep these sequential revisions from contaminating my analysis. Rather I ask what did the principals then believe and know and when did they know it. Given their beliefs and knowledge at the time could they have acted in ways to lower the cost of the war to both sides? Acting differently, however, would have meant giving up the policy models that drove decisions. Ingrained policy models are never revised substantially or abandoned without inner struggle and external political pressure. Unlike scientific models, some decisive experiment cannot be found to refute the model. Even if the empirical parts become falsified over time, the value parts hold policy models together.

So much has been written about the war, with more being written all the time, that I feel obliged to present my warrants for yet another effort. I was in Vietnam several times between 1965 and 1968 as an analyst for the RAND Corporation (now Rand Corporation). My specific job was to show how one could use the ordinary "byproducts" of war—captured documents, prisoners of war interviews, communications intelligence—quantify them, and derive surprising and useful results for strategic and tactical intelligence. This work led directly to a "systems analysis" project on the U.S. war effort. So RAND gave me access to the Pentagon papers (long before Daniel Ellsberg released them to the *New York Times* in June 1971). So I can say that I viewed the intellectual side of the war first from the bottom up and then from the top down from 1961 to 1971 when I left RAND to join the federal government.

This book presents the intellectual history of the war in the United States by contrast and comparison. I will construct the policy models and logic that actors and agents in the war used to motivate their decisions and behavior. To hard scientists and philosophers of science, the term "model" usually implies logically connected, coherent propositions along with accepted procedures and standards for empirical falsification or verification. However, the term "model" that I use in this book means that belief and actions are simply pasted or glued together, with only a messy, partial linkage between them. An incomplete and partial logic connects strongly held beliefs, assumed and verifiable facts, and forecasts that cannot ever be checked out.

Policy models are what decisionmakers offer for the justification behind their actions. Absent such models, we say that the decisionmakers are arbitrary and capricious, a charge that few decisionmakers like to have stick. Alternatively, instead of using the term model, I could have used global strategies, paradigms, appreciations, constructions, frames, cognitive maps, or mind-sets. Besides reconstructing the competing models that decisionmakers and their critics promoted during the war and describing conflicts between models, I have tried to show, within the available historical record, how some models worked out when applied. What I wanted to establish was the relation, if any, between identifiable policy models and the actual conduct of the war.

I know that when bureaucratic actors or agents develop and promote policy arguments, more is always going on than the rational acceptance or rejection of the best substantive ideas or positions. Every policy debate or dispute carries deliberate organizational and personal maneuvers and motivations. Whatever the organizational and personal stakes and motivations, substantive arguments and justifications still have to be offered up for public scrutiny. Arguments and justifications may, of course, be weak or strong, persuasive or unpersuasive, empirically grounded or not. Their quality, in turn, impinges on the latent bureaucratic and personal outcomes. Policy models, held strongly by managers at the top of a bureaucracy, always cascade downwards and sideways. They decide the strategies and behaviors pursued by lower management, and, in turn, condition the intelligence and reporting top management will receive back. Thus, the subject of this book can be viewed, first, as an intellectual story, how different groups thought about the war and the strategic results of their thoughts during the most critical periods of the war, and, second, whether we can improve the thinking of decisionmakers today thrust into similar circumstances. At the very end of the book, I evaluate the potential and the limits of the major analytical, cognitive, and institutional alternatives currently available to improve policy arguments and debate in highly conflicted international crises with irreducible uncertainties *ex ante*, as the Vietnam War turned out to be, and as most other later foreign policy interventions have been.

I caution that the work is not another general descriptive history of the Vietnam War. As agencies release more files, and actors produce more oral and written memoirs, such histories appear regularly, accompanied by the claim, if not the reality, of startling new revelations. Although interpretations differ, that history is by now very well known. However, this book is a history of the strategic and tactical concepts used in arguing about the war, the ideas and concepts that drove the decisions and actions. It is an analysis of how, during the period 1961-1968, different groups of people *thought* about Vietnam: the civilian decisionmakers who made the policies, the military who executed the policies, the various schools of "Doves" who dissented from the policies. For each group, I ask:

- What they thought the national (or world or humanitarian) stake in Vietnam was.

- What they perceived to be the operative factors in world politics and in the Vietnam conflict.

- How they arrived at their views of preferred policy actions.

- For the decisionmakers—the policy actions that they did take; for the critics, the alternatives they proposed and the counterfactual histories they implied.

Harvey Averch
South Miami
March 2002

ACKNOWLEDGMENTS

Gus Shubert, my long time friend and one time colleague at the Rand Corporation in the 1960's and 1970's, an executive in charge of integrating Rand's policy research on Vietnam, provided comment, criticism, and humor when I needed them the most. Despite intermittent illness the last few years, he constantly worked the mail, telephone, and Internet to make this work better.

Helen Turin, my editor at Rand when I worked there, returned from retirement to edit this work. Her familiarity with the structure of policy arguments greatly increased the polish of my presentation this time around.

CHAPTER 1

INTRODUCTION

Since the Vietnam War ended in 1975, many attempts have been made to explain the war and to extract "lessons" for the future. Very large amounts of original source material have appeared. Many more of the principals have had their say on the record, self-justifying as such late testimony may be. However, all the analysis and criticism of the war thus far put on the record, and all the attempts to infer "true" historical lessons, present logical and empirical difficulties. First, the lessons all differ from one another. Second, even if the actual decisionmakers had understood some true *ex post* lesson *ex ante*, they are unlikely to have acted any differently. The U.S. intervention was "overdetermined." It would have taken many powerful lessons collectively heeded to make the United States stay out, or, once having decided to get in, to fight the war differently. Third, the lessons people take away from a war depend on their organizational locus and loyalties during and after the war. For example, the failed "signaling" strategy pursued by the civilian decisionmakers does not imply that higher quality, clearer, even more limited signals should be sent to some adversary in the future. For the U.S. military, the failure means no adversary should ever be given time to reflect after receiving a signal of punishment. Time for strategic reflection after an attack results in the adversary's having time to regain capability, which he will always use. For Doves, it means that any coercive signaling strategy will fail, because only negotiations can be successful.

The early analyses of the Vietnam war explain its causes and the reasons for its persistence in very different terms. Leslie Gelb argues that the war began and persisted because the American bureaucracy continually defined Vietnam to be "vital."[1] Daniel Ellsberg believed that the political interests of the president of the United States caused the war.[2] David Halberstam argued implicitly that the cause of the war and its conduct lay in the character of our national leaders.[3] On the left, Noam Chomsky charged that the cause of the war and its conduct lay in the immorality of national leaders aided and abetted by the immorality of American behavioral scientists.[4]

We usually derive the "lessons" of Vietnam by negating someone else's preferred explanations for the causes of the war and its persistence. For example, if routine bureaucratic behavior caused the United States to escalate into a political and military "quagmire," then such behavior should not go unchecked in the future. Often these *ex post* lessons justify conducting the war in a certain way or ending the war on certain terms. Implicitly, if only decisionmakers had access to some critic's *ex post* lessons and heeded them, then actual outcomes would have been different and better. For example, Admiral Zumwalt, then commander-in-chief of naval forces, argues that the strategy of graduated escalation had

---

1. Gelb (1970, September). Gelb argues that "vitality" was a *sufficient* condition for continued escalation. See also, the later book, Gelb and Betts (1979).

2. See Ellsberg (1970, September).

3. Halberstam, (1971, February). See also Halberstam's previous article on McGeorge Bundy in *Harpers*, January 1969. Halberstam later collected his vignettes as *The Best and the Brightest* (1972). The theme of betrayal and incompetence by U.S. political and social elites carries forward to the present day. See, for example, McMaster (1997).

4. Chomsky (1969).

basic flaws. While the Johnson administration thought it was pursuing a signaling strategy, in fact, General Giap used the pauses to regroup and resupply. Zumwalt asserts that it was McNamara's wilful adoption of the "punish and pause" strategy that caused the "no win" situation.[5]

Thirty-five years after the war began, former Secretary of Defense McNamara himself has tried to prove that the early producers of lessons had them wrong. Even if the United States had heeded all the advice extant at the time, still no satisfactory outcome was possible. McNamara's greatest lesson of all, verified he believes by his personal talks with some North Vietnamese principals in the 1990's, is that neither side understood the other's willingness to inflict and suffer damage. Peace would have had a chance early if only both sides had talked on a deeper level and understood each other's mind-set.[6]

All such *ex post* lessons encounter one major difficulty. They attribute single causes or values motivating those who decided to enter the war and escalate it. Assume escalations were really caused by the inability of the Americans and the North Vietnamese to signal their true willingness to suffer pain. If the signals were sent and correctly read, then both sides would have seized opportunities for an earlier peace. However, both sides had strategic objectives that conflicted. Given the tenacity with which the North Vietnamese held to their objective of unifying the country, the war very likely would have continued, even if the adversaries had understood each others objectives better or perfectly.

---

5. Zumwalt (1997). Zumwalt reports that the Joint Chiefs of Staff wanted a quick invasion of the North with a direct march to Hanoi. The potential for Chinese intervention in this kind of circumstance learned from the Korean War seems to have been forgotten, if the Joint Chiefs really preferred this strategy. Summers (1982) argues that the Chinese used their intervention in Korea as a credible signal to the Americans that too much activity near Hanoi would induce intervention in Vietnam.

6. McNamara (1999). See also McNamara, Blight and Brigham (1995).

Comparisons of the decisionmakers' policy model with the alternative ones presented by the United States military, on the one hand, and those opposed to the war, on the other, are one way to understand the conduct of the war. The military agreed on the values and objectives, but differed on the effectiveness of the instruments the decisionmakers chose to use. Those who opposed the war differed strongly on values but also on the merits of actions and instruments. *To get some lessons that we can use with reasonable confidence, we must understand each part of some policy model supports the other parts. A model is an interlocking network of argument.* Some partial lesson concerning a part of some interlocking model is not likely to be valid or sound. The whole model motivates decisions, not parts.

For example, suppose it were possible to show that immediately before the summer of 1965, when the United States escalated the war, the domino theory was false. Suppose that a U.S. loss would not be seen by the other countries in Southeast Asia as meaning they had now to join the Soviet or the Chinese blocs. Suppose also that North Vietnam had no intention of becoming a proxy for the Soviets or the Chinese. Even such a powerful and decisive proof would, in all likelihood, not have prevented the U.S. escalation. Decisionmakers would simply have switched to another motivating part of their model—for example, making good the word of the United States or the sunk costs already incurred.[7] Policy models are not parsimonious, and decisionmakers can always find some propositions that warrant what they are currently

---

7. Decisionmakers do not ordinarily approach sunk costs the way economists or decision theorists say they should. Sunk costs that appear wasted still have a strong influence on the decisionmakers' reputation for competence. Terminating incomplete, inefficient projects with highly visible sunk costs undermines the future welfare of organizations and decisionmakers. Winning a war with massive waste is always better than losing it efficiently. See Brockner (1992), Averch (1990), and Staw (1976).

doing. Finding plausible justification to continue the war was not difficult, even when decisionmakers knew they were losing. They could always find light at the end of the tunnel for some plausible reason. Even if that light kept receding, their model suggested increased effort should keep the United States moving toward it. Losing itself became a justification for staying in and escalating, a reason like the one that appears in the gambler's ruin paradigm.

Any war, let alone one as complex as the Vietnam War, has many plausible competing lessons. As time passes, new knowledge and events and revised perceptions deliver new lessons or revive old ones. Secretary McNamara's most recent "lessons" operate at such a high level that they seem uncontroversial and not at all derived from the facts and experience of the war. Understanding the mind-set of the adversary is a lesson as old as war itself. So the question is why the highly competent Kennedy-Johnson officials never discovered it. High level communication with the adversary is also ancient.[8] So what institutional or personal barriers prevented the application of this lesson? It was probably the operative policy model the Kennedy-Johnson officials were using. *No proposition exists in this model about any need to talk directly with the adversary.* Certainly, Secretary of State Henry Kissinger, in the succeeding Nixon administration, and grand practitioner of personal diplomacy, had no trouble with high level communication. The lesson may be that high level communication is a necessary condition for settling disputes between adversaries with intensely held, competing values, but it cannot have been sufficient. The war still did not end until 1975 after six years of high level communication.

People who produce "lessons" from history should track their evolution over time before deciding their validity. Over time new conflicts contradict old lessons or reshape them. That such tracking is not an academic exercise is shown by NATO's 1999 armed intervention in Kosovo. Before the intervention, the "lessons" of

---

8. McNamara et al., *op. cit.*, pp. 392-393.

Munich about letting dictators have their way again appeared. The contrary lessons of Vietnam about marching into quagmires were held to be less important. Vietnam teaches us one thing about military interventions on the ground and the 1992 Gulf War another.[9]

Policy models differ from those used in scientific discourse. Very few of the propositions in the former are even potentially refutable. No universally accepted tests falsify or verify them. A model's internal, unfalsifiable propositions sustain it long after its verifiable, factual base may have been eroded or been shown as untrue by experience. Values, rules for action, and preferred instruments are all necessarily derived from the model user's experience before the events that the model will be used to explain. A central question for understanding the substance of decision-making, then, is the match between current models and new events and the ability of a model to cope with new conditions or adapt to them. During the Vietnam war, the decisionmakers' policy model had increasing difficulty explaining and predicting military and civilian outcomes and in generating adequate alternatives to meet changing contingencies. The difficulty can be seen by the constant stream of very high level visitors the decisionmakers sent to Vietnam to find a way to win and in the major reports these visitors wrote between 1961 and 1968. Rather than changing their model, however, or scrapping it, they constantly reinterpreted events to fit the model. The more events invalidated their model, the more they escalated their efforts to validate it.[10] Only a series of major shocks could destroy the model.

The early debates on Vietnam concerned the adequacy of the implicit model the high-ranking civilians used to make the basic

---

9. See Martino (1996) on comparing the lessons of the Viet Nam War and the Gulf War.

10. See the literature on increasing commitment and escalation when decisionmakers become stressed. Staw and Ross (1989).

decisions. Alternatives to the decisionmakers model rarely were articulated well enough so that one could evaluate them on the same scale. The scale to be used was itself problematic. The critics on the left, of course, always held that the scale of judgment was itself a major problem. One way to derive better lessons from history is to make explicit the tacit verbal models of current actors and agents. Later historians can then use them to explain events, review them for consistency, and compare them with available alternatives.[11]

The task of this book will be to identify some of the major policy models, to structure them explicitly where they were left implicit and then to compare their implications for action.[12] The discussion of each model attempts to point out both its logical structure and its empirical statements. Where desired actions rest on beliefs or propositions that are not empirical, as often happens with policy models, I try to point this out. The objective is analytic, to test the models against some of the salient events in Vietnam, not to write another history of the Vietnam War. The intention is to reason about that history from different perspectives and to do so in a formal way.

The "correctness" of a model may or may not relate to the degree of its influence on policy. One lesson of history is that decisionmakers can and do use "incorrect" models. Their models frequently contain inconsistencies among values or objectives, beliefs about the world, the effectiveness of one's own instruments, predicted outcomes, and dispassionately observed reality. However, uncovering such inconsistencies does no necessarily discredit but only calls for reinterpretation.

Inconsistencies showed up early in the decisionmakers' model. However, shaking the strong belief they had in it was still not possible. At least in Vietnam it took two factors working together to shake the model and generate a search for a new one: (1) a

---

11. Meehan (1968).
12. Hambrick (1974).

persistent accumulation of evidence running counter to the model, and (2) exogenous events that made it impossible to ignore or rationalize the cumulated evidence. Once some policy model breaks down, a new one may be very rapidly substituted for the old one. For example, by 1969, "Vietnamization" was at least rhetorically "in." Then, Nixon administration decisionmakers all began speaking of how well the Vietnamization program was going.[13]

During the war, cumulative evidence that the decisionmakers' model was failing did not by itself cause any sustained search for a new model. First, it took a 1967 request by General Westmoreland for an increment of troops so large as to create a difference in kind combined with the surprise 1968 Tet offensive. Then, politically, it took the shock caused by the perceived defeat of President Johnson in the 1968 New Hampshire primary. None of these were sufficient reasons to drop the old model. However, coming on top of the continued drag of outside evidence against the policy model the United States was using, they collectively became sufficient. Inside the government, of course, allegiance to the "standard" model continued to the end and beyond for many principals. For any given strand of a model, one could always argue that not enough had been invested: for example, that the United States did not bomb the North enough rather than accept that bombing could have no decisive effect, given the structure of the Northern economy and polity and the unswerving objectives of the Northern leaders.

---

13. The life cycle for policy models resembles the one postulated by Thomas Kuhn (1970) for scientific models. Kuhn argues that it takes an intellectual crisis of major proportions to force scientists to abandon an old theory and to begin to use a new and more powerful theory. Major theories may be incommensurable in terms of their assumptions, means of verification, and the actual instruments considered acceptable in verification. Using a new conceptual model, even if it is has superior scope and power of explanation, involves heavy "switching costs," as economists call them.

During the Vietnam War finding anyone or any group charged specifically with testing old rules and searching for new ones is difficult.

> The President and his key advisers sought candid assessments of the war, but they would not pay the political costs in terms of friction with the military to get them.... Policy should result from a combination of judgment and analysis, and the best analysis usually comes from adversary proceedings with all interested parties participating. Only then are policymakers likely to see clear alternatives before them, each with its benefits and costs stated as explicitly as possible.... The President and the Secretary of Defense cannot get this kind of analysis simply by asking for it.[14]

Whether the best or even adequate analysis comes from adversary procedures or from some other mode of rational inquiry or whether it comes from appropriate organizational problem solving algorithms is part of our overall discussion. We now know that all modes of analysis and advice-giving and all institutions for analysis and advice-giving are subject to strategic gaming by the participants (Garrison, 1999). There is no intellectual marketplace that automatically clears and presents pragmatically useful, evaluated alternatives for decisionmakers, even highly skeptical ones.

The behavior of the decisionmakers was consistent with a structured policy model that was not amenable to analysis. Its propositions concerned the processes by which one encouraged or deterred conflict, the behavior of allies and adversaries, and the ability of the United States to create competent nations out of apparently poor raw material. A substantive challenge to this model that was adequate to shake it would have had to be delivered on the same grounds. The chapters that follow show challenging

---

14. Enthoven and Smith (1971), p. 307.

policy models on their own terms, using their own logic, are always very difficult.

Chapter 2 contains a brief discussion of the epistemological problems of inferring lessons about Vietnam, or any other conflict for that matter.

Chapters 3, 4, and 5 contain formal statements of the models of Vietnam underlying major policy viewpoints in the United States, along with an analysis of their internal structure. Chapter 3 constructs the model used by civilian decisionmakers in the United States.[15] Chapter 4 describes the model preferred by the U.S. military, showing how doctrine and experience led the military to fight the war with massive amounts of firepower on the ground and in the air. The revealed preferences of most of the military for their firepower model led to conflict with the decisionmakers, signaling strategy and clearly influenced the command and control of the war. For each model, I then draw the implications during three major periods—1961, 1965, and summer 1967 to March 1968. To retain comparability, I have grouped the operational statements in each model into four major common categories—U.S. interests and values, how conflict works politically, how conflict works militarily, how policy is made.

---

15. I have checked this model, where possible, against the much simpler one used by North Vietnamese decisionmakers. See McNamara et al. (1999), *op. cit.* Secretary McNamara reports six sets of meetings with high level North Vietnamese decisionmakers and scholars between 1995 and 1998. He presents actual dialogue with some of these. How much reinterpretation and bolstering of their model the Vietnamese indulged in is hard to establish. McNamara now believes there were lost of opportunities for peace during his tenure, because of major deficiencies in empathy and communications. The unanswered question, not put by Secretary McNamara is why the protagonists should have suffered such a failure in strategic communication, since one of the very well known lessons of history is that miscommunication in war is highly likely and dangerous.

People who believe in a given model will hold propositions in common, but their emphasis will be different. For example, some civilian decisionmakers believed the main purpose of bombing the North was improving the morale and performance of the South Vietnamese government (GVN). Others emphasized coercion against the North to deter it from supplying the Viet Cong. Others believed bombing was a signaling device that the adversary read correctly. However, they all agreed that bombing in the degree tried was necessary. This consensus distinguished the civilian decisionmakers from their Dove critics.

The decisionmakers' model is, of course, the central one. It is the only one that was operational on the ground. It sets the frame for the questions that everyone else posed about the war. The military and the Doves constructed alternatives to replace the central decisionmakers' model in part or whole. The military chafed under the constraints imposed by the decisionmakers. Throughout the war, the military believed that not enough force was being applied. Refuting the decisionmakers' model, proving first that it was morally flawed or, if not, then empirically unsound, preoccupied Doves of all stripes.

Chapter 6 compares the major alternatives for evaluating policy. It contains a discussion of the algorithms and procedures for constructing policy models, *ex ante*. For example questions of fact and value were greatly tangled by all the parties in the Vietnam debate. Are there any means to introduce clearer warrants for action or not? What is the role of technical analysis within a policy debate? Enthoven and Smith's discussion of analysis on the war (done within the government) suggests that analysis was primarily concerned with efficiency questions *after* the strategic issues were decided.[16] Evidence and research were not often used in the formulation of strategy proper, although it was used in prosecuting the war.[17] The same seems true of research on Vietnam overall.

---

16. See in Enthoven and Smith, *op. cit.*, pp. 267-308.
17. See Webb (1968).

Clearly, assertions, beliefs, and predictions about outcomes played a major role. Given that there are no persuasive validity tests, a major problem of information for decision making arises.

It may be true, as Assistant Secretary of Defense John McNaughton once wrote, that problems of policy do not respond to any test of objective fact, but only to the test of informed judgment. Nevertheless, having a test for informed judgment is necessary, for many competitors claim to have it. This claim raises the problem of testing or accounting for the predictions people make.

If a priori, rational kinds of inquiry cannot do the job of critically reviewing *ex ante* policy models, then it may be we have to improve individual decisionmaking protocols or instititutionalize organizations that learn and that can meliorate flawed decisions by their members. Chapter 6 evaluates these approaches by comparing applied prospect theory to improve individual decisions and organizational algorithms designed to overcome unimproved decisionmaking.[18]

The kind of analysis I use for the Vietnam War models has been used in other contexts. For example, in strategic nuclear debates, occurring at the same time as the Vietnam War and involving the same decisionmakers, competing models of deterrence were subjected to close, almost Talmudic scrutiny, within the government and outside. At least those decisionmakers and analysts involved established where they differed, and why. The same kind of knowledge is the aim of this book.

---

18. Prospect theory describes how people actually behave as compared to a rational ideal of expected global utility maximization under uncertainty. So an applied prospect theory is one that helps correct for mental "error" in making subjective probability estimates, in framing definition of gains and losses, and for real, empirically-derived utility functions that reveal non-convexities in shape. The mental errors and the "strange" utility functions lead to risk prone behavior when people are losing and risk-averse behavior when they are "winning." For a large scale survey of the entire field, see Kahneman and Twersky (2000).

CHAPTER 2

EVIDENCE AND INFERENCE CONCERNING VIETNAM DECISIONMAKING

The unit of analysis in this study is a *policy model*, a loosely connected set of propositions believed in by an identifiable group of actors involved in setting policy on the war. In reality, multiple individual decisionmakers, generals, and Doves had their own perspectives and preferences. However, they arranged themselves in distributions around the propositions in a model. These distributions are characterized here by aggregate propositions as rough measures of central tendencies. Distributions have means and medians, and so constructing models is meaningful relative to their central tendencies. For example, Doves are always much closer to each other than to decisionmakers. In statistical language the between-group variation seems much larger than the within-group variations.

A different kind of analysis, and a harder one, would be to obtain the entire distribution of positions for a group and to explain the distribution. That type of analysis could try to explain a particular actor's preferred policy model relative to his place in the organization or relative to his personality type. Then, given the competing models of all the individuals we could show how the organization came to prefer a single model from all those available to it. Neither the data nor any persuasive analytical scheme supports such an analysis.[1]

Some of the documentary evidence of the time was originally classified. Decision memos and reports in bureaucracies are created to persuade and to "win" people around to one's own policy positions. What one puts on paper in a war of memos may have only a proximate relationship to true beliefs and true reasons for action. One way to check the classified discussions of the time is to compare them with what the decisionmakers and generals were saying in public at the same time. In fact, the private models presented in classified memoranda, reports, and assessments are remarkably consistent with the ones presented to the public as the justification for entering and widening the war. The decisionmakers in private were truly desperate about the domino theory, about dominos falling and often said so in public.

Besides using the then classified documents of the decisionmakers and the military, this study also uses statements about events extracted from journalists, columns and interviews or from analytical news accounts. These were taken from a large group of open documents called the "Vietnam package" collected by The Rand Corporation beginning in 1965. The rules for collection were as follows:

---

1. Steinberg (1996) argues that different presidential personalities would have made a difference in the conduct of the Vietnam War. Johnson, allegedly, stayed to avoid "humiliation," and Nixon kept us in because of low self-esteem. Eisenhower was more psychologically secure and so felt comfortable keeping the nation out of Vietnam when he had a chance to go in. However, decisions to go in or stay out can be explained without appeal to the psychological makeup of the people who made the decisions. The decisions are overdetermined, since many plausible explanations are available that would produce the same result. It takes a long and tenuous chain of reasoning to get from a president's personality to an organizational decision to go to war.

1. There was an attempt to include major policy statements by major policymakers, for example, the president, secretaries of State and Defense, the military leadership, and the Congressional leadership.

2. The overall aim was balanced coverage, in regional and philosophical terms, for example, the *Atlanta Constitution* as well as the *St. Louis Post Dispatch,* the *Nation* magazine columnists on the left and Joseph Alsop on the right. The one exception to this rule was the omission of a representative West Coast newspaper, the reasoning being that readers could clip their own *Los Angeles Times*.

3. Never to include wire service dispatches, which represent spot coverage; most articles are either editorials or byline analysis.

A different kind of problem occurs with respect to the military and Dove models, since neither were ever implemented. History provides no direct tests of these models and their role in decisions. We then move into the problem of using counterfactual policy arguments based on plausible, but fictional counterhistory.

The problem of making valid counterfactual propositions in history itself has a long history. Some argue that no counterfactual proposition can ever be proved, since the evidence for the proof must always be taken from the real world. Others argue that to the extent history is a science, explanation consists of specifying and testing "causal" models. Counterfactuals come about by manipulating variables in a model. They are predictions and no more easy or difficult to make than nontemporal ones based on multivariate statistical analysis. Good predictions depend upon the proper specification of a model.[2]

---

2. For the range of debate, see Fischer (1970) and Fogel (1970). For modern discussion, see, for example, Demandt (1993), Tetlock and Belkin (1996), and Jentleson (2000).

Specification tests do not exist for counterfactual policy models the way they do for cliometric models. Even so, we can examine their logical and empirical warrants, the predictions found in them, and their importance in public debate. The expansive military model described in Chapter 4 and the Dove models discussed in Chapter 5 provide "boundary" conditions and constraints on the actual models being used by the decisionmakers. Alternatives are always waiting in the wings when some model is being tested in action. The available alternatives and their credibility condition how hard an actual model will be pushed.

CHAPTER 3

THE CIVILIAN DECISIONMAKERS' MODEL

In Vietnam, the decisionmakers' policy model filtered and altered the operational meaning of current events to fit very strong beliefs constructed along ago. This chapter first specifies a policy model that has significant "explanatory power" for the way civilian decisionmakers approached political and military events in Vietnam. This model helps explain the major decisions and the advice leading up to the decisions. Its logical and empirical structures show why refuting it proved very difficult. Connecting the model with decisions and events tests it for "goodness of fit" with actual behavior using the qualitative data contained in the Vietnam literature. The evidence supports the specification and use of this model or some variant of it.

Although the United states had been involved in Vietnam since World War II, for analytical convenience, we begin in 1961. Just like any other problem, foreign or domestic, Vietnam only periodically received sustained attention. Many country-specific issues always compete for the attention of top decisionmakers and lower level foreign policy officials. Unless there is a crisis, the probability of any single country receiving constant attention is low. Before 1961, cross-sectional, year by year analysis of American foreign policy would show that Vietnam received low priority and attention, except in 1954 when President Eisenhower faced a French request for assistance at Dien Bien Phu, a request he denied.

> International crises are relative phenomena in Washington, as they are in every world capital. Thus during President Eisenhower's second term, little attention was paid to developments in Vietnam or Laos, until it became abundantly and depressingly clear that the regimes of Ngo Dinh Diem in Vietnam and Phoumi Nosavan in Laos were both in serious trouble.[1]

The decisionmakers and their principal advisers believed they already possessed a valid general model concerning the appropriate behavior for the United States, its allies, and its adversaries. Initially they had no reason to try to single out Vietnam as any different from other postwar involvements. The United States had been involved in crises that could be and were formulated as directly analogous to Vietnam. In Greece and the Philippines, the United States had helped defeat indigenous insurgencies. Britain, a major ally, had successfully defeated an insurgency on the Asian continent in Malaya. The Berlin blockade, Korea, the Quemoy-Matsu crisis, and other cold war confrontations had also been resolved satisfactorily, if not as one sided in favor of the United States as some wanted. There was little incentive in the beginning to try to differentiate Vietnam from other successfully managed crises in the past.

THE DECISIONMAKERS' MODEL

The following *ex ante* model or paradigm that the civilian decisionmakers applied in Vietnam does not explain all the decisions made, but it does have substantial explanatory power with respect to the "macro" behavior of the United States.

---

1. Cooper (1970), p. 164.

Decisionmakers deployed the models a priori propositions at three critical times: 1961, 1965, and summer 1967 to March 1968. The model contains 14 propositions grouped into four categories U.S values and interests, how insurgency conflicts work politically, how they work militarily, and how policy is made.[2]

A. United States Values and Interests

DM1. *The conflict between communists and noncommunists (i.e., the "Free World" plus the "Third World") is a conflict over the control of nation-states. A gain for the communists implies some loss for the United States.* (This differs from an earlier Dulles formulation that a loss for the "Free World," including a loss to the "Third World," implied a gain for the communists).

DM2. Domino proposition: *The probability of additional communist gains rises after even a single gain.*

Alternate DM2. Geographic domino proposition: *The probability of additional communist gains increases particularly strongly in countries near one gained by the communists.*

DM3. *The morale, confidence, and behavior of other nations in resisting communism rise and fall in response to U.S. efforts at resistance.* If the United States does not resist, then other nations will become easier targets for communist adversaries or will allow the communists to gain control.

DM3.1 Corollary: *There exists a national interest based on confrontation itself.* This kind of proposition about national interest is quite different from "classically" asserted ones derived from geography or access to resources. What is important is a test of U.S. will against that of her adversaries.

DM4. "Sunk cost" proposition: *After some effort to resist communism, the anticipated costs to the United States of disengag-*

---

2. The propositions in the decisionmakers' model will be denoted as DM.

*ing from further action rise according to the size of the effort
previously exerted as measured by the future calculations and behavior of allies and adversaries and by expected domestic political
difficulties.*

   DM5. *Whenever the United States forecasts that an ally is
unable to contain or defeat communist insurgency, the United
States must attempt to defeat it.*

This proposition can be derived from Propositions DM3 and
DM4. If an increased flow of U.S resources is small in relation to
potentially available resources, the United States should act to
avoid the outcomes listed in Proposition DM3. Such outcomes
will, in turn, increase the probability of communist gains (Proposition DM2). After some increased resource flows have occurred,
additional resources are necessary to avoid the increased costs of
stopping action (Proposition DM4).

B. How Insurgency Conflicts Work Politically

   DM6. *Inputs from a contiguous communist nation are a
necessary condition for the success of communist insurgency.*
Proposition DM6 can be stated in a stronger form: *Unless external
inputs are prevented, then even an effective ally and substantial
commitment of U.S. forces will lead to stalemate at best.*

   DM7. *An adversary will recognize the positive relation
between additional U.S. resource inputs and increased U.S. will
and commitment.* If DM7 were true, the United States could send
clear signals that an external communist nation supporting an
insurgency in some ally of the United States would suffer high
levels of damage in the future if that nation continued its support
by stepping up resource flows to its ally.[3]

---

   3. At that time the scholarly literature suggested that since stable
mutual deterrence now held at the strategic level, then limited wars had
truly to be limited. Limited war was now a craft of signaling,

DM8. *A positive relationship exists between United States resource inputs to an ally and the U.S. ability to endow the ally with high morale and competence.* Without such U.S. inputs, a typical third world government can be expected to be weak and disorganized.

DM9. *Neither military force nor political effort suffices to defeat insurgency. Both are necessary in an unspecified mix.*

DM10. *In political efforts to win popular support, the first requirement is security against terrorism; the second is western-style efficiency and political democracy; the third, economic and social reform such as land reform.* In case of conflict among the three requirements, security takes priority. The third is particularly difficult to achieve and may be politically destabilizing.

DM11. *The behavior of government toward its population will be changed by changing the ally's political institutions and civilian and military bureaucracies.* Eventually, efficient allied organizations will carry out the substantive programs that will induce popular support.[4]

Experience, however, provided no clear doctrine concerning the levels (provincial, village) at which reorganization was needed, or how it was to spread from level to level.

Converse to Proposition DM11 (frequently believed simultaneously):

---

bargaining, and indirect negotiation designed to influence an adversary to select an option preferred by the United States. See Schelling (1960), and Schelling (1966). This view assumed that the adversary could read the signal and really cared about what you were saying.

4. Americans usually assume that when the formal institutions and processes of representative government are introduced, they will work as they do in the West. Representative institutions respond to the population's perceived needs for changes in economic, social, and political conditions. See the discussion of American political attitudes in Almond and Verba (1963).

DM11 Converse: *But do not rock the boat in which you have elected to sail.*

C. How Insurgency Conflicts Work Militarily

DM12. *The U.S. military establishment had evolved or could easily evolve an effective strategy and force structure for conducting military operations in conventional and insurgent environments as well as for controlling the signal content of these operations.*

DM12.1 Organizational corollary: *There is little need for civilian decisionmakers to concern themselves with the effective use of military resources in war time.*

DM13. *Graduated military escalation is an effective way to achieve compliance by an adversary to U.S.-preferred behavior, though such escalation will stop well short of a level that might bring in China or the Soviet Union.*

D. How Policy Is Made

DM14. Incrementalism as desired process: *Policy is made and changed incrementally. Changes in direction will be gradual and difficult to achieve. If decisions do not have to be made, they should not be made.*

THE STRUCTURE OF THE MODEL

As is clear (with hindsight) from the statement of the model, and as demonstrated later in this chapter, the model did not apply very well or very fully to Vietnam. However, for a long time, opponents of the war found it impossible to shake the decisionmakers' faith in it in any fundamental way. Why? The answer lies in the logic and the structure of the model; large parts are simply not subject to refutation. An examination of the 14 propositions shows that they consist of statements of value, statements concerning asserted existing relations (facts), action implications derived from the value statements and the facts, and predictions concerning outcomes. For example, Proposition DM1 is a statement of value on "Free World" and communist gains and losses for some asserted U.S. national interest. In contrast, Proposition DM11 is a statement of factual relationships between government organization and performance within a country. At least in theory, a (costly) test for it could be devised.

The "domino" proposition DM2 is a contingent prediction about the actions of other nations. A deliberate test of the proposition is excluded, because it would consist of allowing the unfortunate contingency to occur, and keeping close watch on future events. However, the purpose of action is to support the first domino and prevent it from falling.[5]

Since no direct tests of predictions about falling dominoes could be made, they were justified by historical analogies or historical "lessons." It is not surprising that Vietnam has over the years been compared with Munich, Korea, Greece, Algeria, and Cuba.[6] Although there is no test of DM2-type propositions, there were "indicators" that reinforced belief in their soundness. For example, U.S. diplomats and decisionmakers frequently ask decisionmakers in other nations to forecast what will happen in their own country if U.S. efforts to assist country X turn out to be inadequate. Intelligence and information analysts then process and count forecasts and then offer them as ostensibly factual (but still irrefutable) assertions for use by decisionmakers. In the early sixties, if these personal forecasts contained statements about loss

---

5. Vietnam fell to the communists in 1975, and most of the projected dominoes still have not fallen 25 years later, providing a partial test of the proposition. However, no year 2000 test was available in 1961.

6. See Fischer (1970) for a discussion of the use of analogy with examples from Vietnam, p. 248. See Khong (1992).

to the United States, they were defined as having provided sufficient "evidence" about the importance of stemming any communist insurgency.

Overall, then, Propositions DM1-DM5 are all irrefutable. Although they use some predictive structure that might be tested, the predictions are contingent upon the violation of asserted (and untestable) value statements of U.S. interests. To test the predictive portions would do violence to the interests; therefore, there are no tests.

Propositions DM6-DM11 are factual and predictive, with less value content, and, therefore, might be tested. Nevertheless, the model does not contain any "feedback" or evaluation rule. There is no internal proposition for modifying behavior after a reasonable empirical test of the propositions.[7] Proposition DM4—that sunk costs raise stakes—makes it very difficult to incorporate any such evaluation rules. For commitment enhances the original values implying that instruments should be applied more heavily. The difference in the approach to sunk costs between a policy domain and a quasi-scientific field can be illustrated by juxtaposing statements on sunk costs, first by Paul Samuelson using the guidance of economic theory, and then by Henry Kissinger.

> The economist always stresses the "extra" or "marginal" costs and advantages of any decision ... let bygones be bygones. Don't look backward. Don't moan about your sunk costs. Look forward.[8]

> However fashionable it is to ridicule the terms "credibility" or "prestige," they are not empty phrases: other nations can gear their actions to ours only if they can count on our steadiness. The

---

7. No reasonable test is possible for some, because any negative result of the test means that the strategy is correct but has not been applied intensively enough.

8. The same view persists in modern microeconomic texts. Samuelson (1964), pp. 482-483.

collapse of the American effort in Vietnam would not mollify
many critics ... [*and*] Those whose safety or national goals
depend on American commitments could only be dismayed. In
many parts of the world ... stability depends on confidence in
American promises.[9]

Continuous evaluation of even those propositions that are concep-
tually testable is thus rendered difficult.

Time presents even more difficulty, since it does not enter into
the decision calculus in any explicit way. The predictions are not
tagged with any estimates about how long they will take to be
realized. Nor are there explicit time estimates in the factual
assertions concerning the effectiveness of one's own instruments—
here, U.S. resources. Even if there were a set of evaluation rules,
evaluators would be hard pressed to say when a proposition had
been given a fair chance to operate—two years, five years, or ten
years?

Another general characteristic of this model is that it is
aggregate in nature. Its propositions are about conflicts between
nation-states and about how nation-states influence another. The
model is not very specific about group interactions within these
nation-states, about the distribution of behavior within their
governments, or about the interactions between governments and
their populations. For example, Proposition DM8 states that the
United States can create a national government that is both
effective and willing to combat insurgents. It is not about the
process by which U.S. resources affect or do not affect the fine-
grained organizational arrangements within a country. Propositions
DM10 and DM11 get below nation level with their assertions
about needed changes in national operational modes, but only in
terms of gross structural relationships—for example, "security

---

9. *Foreign Affairs* (1969, January), p. 219. Kissinger may be using
a complementary version of the economist's concept of sunk costs. At
the margin, it may pay to go ahead and finish some job once started.

first"—that move little beyond the whole-nation assertions of Proposition DM8.

Aggregation is, of course, both inevitable and necessary in a policy model. Decisionmakers cannot inundate themselves with hundreds or thousands of facts, propositions, and predictions. The question is the proper level of aggregation and how to test for the sensitivity of the propositions to aggregation. For example, at least until the major escalation in 1965, the word "leverage" was fashionable in Vietnam. The United States, a nation-state, would apply leverage by using its economic, military, and political instruments to induce the GVN, another nation-state, to induce its component organizations to behave in a U.S.-preferred way (Proposition DM8). Presumably the component organizations would then act to induce the whole population to behave in a U.S.-preferred way. However, this says nothing about the attenuation of leverage as one attempts to influence larger and larger numbers of smaller and smaller units.

The interaction among all the propositions in the model creates a cohesive structure that is difficult to refute. This is another characteristic of policy models. Some isolated empirical parts of the model may be refuted by analysis of particular propositions; some of the aggregate empirical propositions rest on implicit propositions about low-level interactions that can be tested. However, to address the propositions in their own terms at their own levels, it is necessary to argue by analogy that is difficult to make persuasive. One is forced into arguments about similarity and dissimilarity where there is little control on relevant variables. Alternatively, one could argue on some statistical basis that is again difficult to make persuasive because of inadequate data and method.

Testing predictions is possible, in principle, based on projected factual outcomes. If such predictions were recorded, we could keep score on the successful and the unsuccessful ones. A factual proposition giving mostly unsuccessful predictions would then be thrown into question. In practice, of course, few decisionmakers or analysts dare risk recording bold predictions. The perceived penalties for being wrong, even after using the best available information and techniques, are too high—at least as our current policymaking organizations are set up.[10]

Although we can discuss the merits of value propositions about the national interest, there is no way to refute them. (Part of the inquiry later in this study is to compare the value propositions of different models). Value judgments can be weighed explicitly against competing values. However, a case for abandoning a model derived from its values would have to become politically potent. The maintained values in the model would have to be subject to great public stress. Large amounts of cumulative evidence that the factual assertions are unsound with major exogenous shocks may combine with value systems competing for dominance. This can cause decisionmakers to abandon or change a model. I believe this happened in 1967-1968.

The following three sections test the 14-proposition model by explaining some major events in terms of the logic of its propositions. The final section will illustrate the shocks that logic suffered, leading to a partial abandonment of the model in March 1968.

The Logic of Intervention, 1961

In 1961 concerns over Vietnam were derived from other crises, and actions in Vietnam had less to do with local events than with losing and the fear of losing in Cuba, Berlin, and Laos. In particu-

---

10. This may suggest some need for an institutionalized, highly placed, and well-staffed devil's advocate. This was a role sometimes attributed to George Ball during the war. Ball, however, was neither institutionalized or staffed; and his predictions and propositions about Vietnam presumably had no stronger proofs than the predictions and propositions he wanted to refute. Thus, he was used as a symbol of in-house criticism and then ignored. The decisionmakers would work out scenarios before meetings, let Ball speak in opposition, and then proceed to the actions that had been agreed before the meeting, giving the appearance that a vigilant decision process was at work.

lar, if Laos fell, then the potential loss of Vietnam increased both in likelihood (a geographical version of domino Proposition DM2) and in cost to the United States (Proposition DM4, sunk costs increase future stakes).

Khrushchev's speech on January 6, 1961 promising Soviet support for wars of liberation in Cuba, Vietnam, and Algeria clinched the President-elect's determination to move ahead on counter-insurgency program.[11]

The President, too, reacted to the Bay of Pigs failure, but in the opposite direction. He had refused to use American troops to invade Cuba because he did not want to pay the political cost of using the overwhelming American power against a small nation that was not in fact a threat to American security. But it seemed possible that the communists might see his decision as irresolution.[12]

As the dreary spring of 1961 pushed toward its close, there was a growing fatalism that whatever happened at the Laos Conference the Communists rather than the West would probably come out on top in Laos ... But the reasoning went, the West, (i.e., the United States) would nevertheless have to make a strong stand against Communist expansion in Southeast Asia; if the Laotians did not have the courage and determination to warrant American support, the Vietnamese—a tougher, more energetic and more strongly motivated people—would have to be relied on.[13]

In the spring of 1961 the administration worked up a counterinsurgency program estimated as adequate to handle the current Viet Cong threat in the South.[14] Although the issue of committing

---

11. Cooper (1970), p. 174.
12. Hilsman (1967), p. 134.
13. Cooper, *op. cit.*, pp. 177-178.
14. Interdepartmental Task Force. (1961, May 8). A Program of Action for South Vietnam. In *Pentagon Papers* (1971), pp. 637-642.

American troops certainly vexed the decisionmakers throughout 1961, the issue was deferred until after the fall mission of General Maxwell Taylor and Walt Rostow (Proposition DM14, when possible, decisions are deferred). In the fall of 1961 the additional inputs recommended by Taylor and Rostow after their visit did not really differ in kind from those discussed earlier except that they recommended a small troop commitment of 8000. The arguments for troop deployment were put in terms of signals to the adversary and to the GVN (DM7 and DM8). According to Taylor.

> In Vietnam "and Southeast Asia" there is a double crisis in confidence: doubt that United States is determined to save Southeast Asia; doubt that Diem's methods can frustrate and defeat Communist purposes and methods. The Vietnamese (and Southeast Asians) will undoubtedly draw—rightly or wrongly— definitive conclusions in coming weeks and months concerning the probable outcome and will adjust their behavior accordingly. What the United States does or fails to do will be decisive to the end result.[15]

Based on the Taylor-Rostow report, Secretary McNamara concluded that, in the worst case, about six U.S. divisions would be needed.

> If we act in this way, the ultimate possible extent of our military commitment must be faced. The struggle may be prolonged and Hanoi and Peiping may intervene overtly. In view of the logistic difficulties faced by the other side, I believe we can assume that the maximum United States forces required on the ground in Southeast Asia will not exceed 6 divisions, or about 205,000 men (CINCPAC Plan 32-59, Phase IV). Our military posture is, or with the addition of more National Guard or regular Army

---

15. Taylor, M. Gen. (1961, November 1). Document #27: Cablegram to President Kennedy. In Sheehan et al. (1971), p. 144.

divisions, can be made, adequate to furnish these forces without serious interference with our present Berlin plans.[16]

This upper bound estimate on the worst contingency was accepted by the administration (Proposition DM12, strategy and force structure were appropriate). It is hard to find evidence that any special characteristics of the GVN or Viet Cong organizations received much attention in the early counterinsurgency plan or in the Taylor-Rostow report. U.S. plans and instruments were general and could have been applied in many places, standard economic aid for nation-building and military assistance to help an ally's military capabilities. The analogies drawn were to successful counterinsurgencies—Greece, Malaya, the Philippines. Knowing that success required both military and political input was sufficient (Proposition DM9). There was little discussion as to tradeoffs between measures and the degree to which previous analogies would hold.

> Magsaysay's campaign against the Hukbalahaps in the Philippines provided a model: tough counter guerrilla action, generous provision for amnesty, real and sweeping political and economic reforms.[17]

Although decisionmakers believed an extended struggle was imminent in Vietnam, they had no doubt that the United States had the will and the means to carry out such a struggle. The situation appeared retrievable. The United States had helped allies in counterinsurgency actions before.

The model does not contain any proposition concerning political reaction in the United States to prolonged warfare. Contemporaneous thinking about such warfare did not consider

---

16. McNamara, R. S. (1961, November 8). Document #29: Memorandum for the President from Secretary of Defense. In Sheehan et al. (1971), p. 149.

17. Schlesinger, *op. cit.*, p. 541.

domestic political reaction.[18] That the French effort in Indochina had overturned a government and the counterinsurgency effort in Algeria had overthrown a regime went unnoted.

The importance of carrying on even a lengthy struggle in Vietnam was unquestioned by the civilian decisionmakers (Proposition DM5, the national interest in defeating any communist insurgency).

> The deteriorating situation in South Viet-Nam requires attention to the nature and scope of United States national interests in that country. The loss of South Viet-Nam to Communism would involve the transfer of a nation of 20 million people from the free world to the Communist bloc. The loss of South Viet-Nam would make pointless any further discussion about the importance of Southeast Asia to the free world; we would have to face the near certainty that the remainder of Southeast Asia and Indonesia would move to a complete accommodation with Communism, if not formal incorporation with the Communist bloc. The United States, as a member of SEATO, has commitments with respect to South Viet-Nam under the Protocol to the SEATO Treaty. Additionally, in a formal statement at the conclusion session of the 1954 Geneva Conference, the United States representative stated that the United States "would view any renewal of the aggression ... with grave concern and seriously threatening international peace and security."
>
> The loss of South Viet-Nam to Communism would not only destroy SEATO but would undermine the credibility of American commitments elsewhere. Further, loss of South Viet-Nam would stimulate bitter domestic controversies in the United States and would be seized upon by extreme elements to divide the country and harass the Administration...[19]

---

18. McNamara believed that the public would support a decisive early effort rather than a graduated escalation punctuated by casualties. Halperin (1963) contained a two page discussion.

19. Rusk, D. and MacNamara, R. S. (1961, November 11). Document #30: Report to Kennedy on South Vietnam. In Sheehan et al.

This single statement unites almost the entire set of propositions, DM1 through DM5, containing the decisionmakers' cold war view of the U.S. national interest. It also includes other propositions that define their view on how this national interest could be exerted. The operation of the geographic version of the domino theory (Proposition DM2) raised the stakes to the point where the confrontation in itself was necessary (Proposition DM3). If the United States lost its will, it could lose all of Asia.

To avoid this possibility, then, supplying additional resources to Vietnam was necessary. This would signal resolve and commitment to our enemies in Vietnam (Proposition DM7), to our allies there (Proposition DM8), and more generally, around the world (Proposition DM3). U.S. commitments in Vietnam would help restore the confidence and morale lost by the cold war setbacks of 1961 (Proposition DM4: *not* increasing sunk costs sends bad signals). American ability to translate confidence and morale into concrete behavior by a government like that of Vietnam depended on U.S. resource inputs (Proposition DM8). In 1961 the insurgency was perceived as only partially indigenous. It stemmed primarily from the covert aggression of the North (Proposition DM6: successful communist insurgencies require outside help). According to Hillsman:

> A major attack was being launched. It was indirect, but still it was aggression—through the guerrilla tactics and techniques of "internal war."[20]

Hillsman also cites Rostow's retroactively famous 1961 speech on counterinsurgency that emphasized that the North and South were two nations. A new form of aggression was "...sending men

---

(1971), p. 150.
20. Hillsman, *op. cit.*, p. 419.

and arms across international boundaries and the direction of guerrilla war from outside a sovereign nation."[21]

But though the United States gave very heavy weight to the potential role of North Vietnam, it was perceived as currently providing limited support. At the currently perceived level of Northern support, the GVN could suppress the insurgency if its effectiveness were increased by U.S. aid.

> In 1961 all the evidence was not yet in on the extent to which the anti-government forces in the South were the creatures of the communist North. But it was reasonably clear that many of them were trained in the North, armed and supplied by the North, and infiltrated from the North through the Laotian corridors ... The North supplied a considerable degree of coordination and control.[22]

Continued or increased Northern support, however, implied that it would be very difficult to suppress an insurgency that had assistance from a contiguous communist neighbor. A necessary condition for insurgent success, according to Proposition DM6—was coming very close to being a sufficient condition for such success.

> The introduction of a United States force of the magnitude of an initial 8,000 men in a flood relief context will be of great help to Diem. However, it will not convince the other side (whether the shots are called from Moscow, Peiping, or Hanoi) that we mean business. Moreover, it probably will not tip the scales decisively. We would be almost certain to get increasingly mired down in an inconclusive struggle.
>
> The other side can be convinced we mean business only if we accompany the initial force introduction by a clear commitment to the full objective stated above, accompanied by a warning through some channel to Hanoi that continued support

21. *Ibid*, p. 422.
22. Sorenson, (1965), *op. cit.*, p. 650.

of the Viet Cong will lead to punitive retaliation against North Vietnam.[23]

Either way, however, necessary or sufficient, the Northern aggression could be used to justify U.S. action against the North.

> They [Taylor and Rostow] therefore raised the question of how long Saigon and the United States could be expected to play by the existing ground rules, which permitted North Vietnam to train and supply guerillas from across the border and denied South Vietnam the right to strike back at the source of aggression.[24]

The North's motivation for its aggression is left ambiguous, an ambiguity that was tolerable to the decisionmakers in 1961. For the North counted mainly as the instrument of the communist forces in a confrontation with Asia-wide and, perhaps, worldwide implications. Proposition DM3, requiring U.S. resolve in a global contest really carried weight. Sometimes relative failure in the North was emphasized as motivating the immediate aggression; the intervention in the South was blamed on a growing gap between the South and the North.

> But, as his own economy faltered in comparison with Diem's ... as the militancy of Red China gained ascendance in his own camp, the "struggle for national reunification," as Ho called it ...began in earnest.[25]

> Living standards, indeed, had risen faster in South Vietnam than in North Vietnam, where Ho Chi Minh concentrated on investment rather than consumption. ...as the success of Diem's

---

23. McNamara, R. S. (1961, November 8). Document #29: Memorandum for the President from Secretary of Defense. In Sheehan et al. (1971), p. 149.
24. Schlesinger (1965), p. 546.
25. Sorenson, *op.cit.*, p. 650.

economic policies convinced Ho Chi Minh that he could not wait passively for the Diem regime to collapse, he sent word to his comrades in the South to join the guerrillas.[26]

At other times reference is made to the innate ambitions of North Vietnam:

No amount of social and economic assistance in South Vietnam would end the ambitions of North Vietnam.[27]

Writing retrospectively in 1967, however, William Bundy attributed both a much deeper and stronger 1961 motive to the North, and a much deeper understanding to the United States decisionmakers of that time.

We knew that the action against South Vietnam reflected Hanoi's deeply held ambitions to unify Vietnam under communist control.[28]

In fact, the differences in the motives attributed to the North did not seem highly relevant at the time. In retrospect they appear quite important. If the real motive for the aggression were economic jealousy, and if social and economic assistance made South Vietnam grow faster, then such assistance would increase the gap between the North and South, creating even greater incentives for aggression. However, aggression thus motivated could be countered by increasing the cost to the North, and this would provide a specifically Vietnamese content for Proposition DM13 on the uses of escalation. If, however, American decisionmakers had accepted the much deeper national unity motivations mentioned by Bundy, both Proposition DM13 (on escalation as a device to compel political compliance) and Proposition DM7 (on United States

---

26. Schlesinger, *op. cit*, p. 538.
27. Sorenson, *op. cit.*, p. 656.
28. Bundy (1967), p. 655.

signals to the enemy) would have been thrown into question. This in turn could have raised serious questions about both the model and the effort as a whole.

THE GVN SUSCEPTIBILITY

These arguments, concerned the external assistance that, according to Proposition DM6, was necessary for serious insurgency. What also had to be explained was the susceptibility of the South to such insurgency. The model would attribute this to the unpopularity of the Diem regime. Unpopularity, in turn, depended on the failure to provide internal security, a necessary condition for political and economic development, according to Proposition DM10. In 1961, the Viet Cong was at best a shadowy organization. Whatever popular appeal it had rested more on the Diem regime's failures than on the Viet Cong's own programs. Viet Cong control in the countryside was attributed primarily to fear and coercion made possible by the GVN's security failures:

> The Viet Cong unquestionably expressed a strain of fanatic idealism.... Nationalists fought side by side with communists. But the Viet Cong did not precisely represent a movement of rural uplift. They extended their power as much by the fear they incited as by the hope they inspired.
>
> Still, the systematic murder of village officials ... could be an effective weapon too....[29]

The peasant population, apathetic to a central government of whatever character, was becoming increasingly alienated as a result of Saigon's failure to supply the only service that every village and hamlet expected of it—security from attack. Land reform, tax reform, fertilizer programs, added up only to slogans—which in the far too many cases they turned out to be

---

29. Schlesinger (1965), *op. cit.*, p. 539.

—unless the farmers could plant their seed and harvest their crops unmolested.[30]

That a policy of selective assassination could generate political popularity was not initially within the decisionmakers' perceptions.

As far as the grievances about the GVN proper (besides failure to provide security) were concerned, their major negative effects were perceived as relating more to the lack of political democracy than to failure to satisfy the population's economic or social desires. This fits the hierarchy and priorities in Proposition DM10. The basic political grievance was defined as the unrepresentative nature of the Diem government. The administration decided to induce much more representation by aid conditional on reform.

> ...Clear the air—Diem should get everyone back to work and get them to focus on winning the war. He should be broad-minded and compassionate in his attitude toward those who have, for understandable reasons, found it difficult under recent circumstances fully to support him. A real spirit of reconciliation could work wonders on the people he leads; a punitive, harsh or autocratic attitude could only lead to further resistance.
>
> B. Buddhists and students—Let them out and leave them unmolested. This more than anything else would demonstrate the return of a better day and the refocusing on the main job at hand, the war.
>
> C. Press—The press should be allowed full latitude of expression. Diem will be criticized, but leniency and cooperation with the domestic and foreign press at this time would bring praise for his leadership in due course. While tendentious reporting is irritating, suppression of news leads to much more serious trouble.
>
> D. Secret and combat police—Confine its role to operations against the VC and abandon operations against non-Communist opposition groups thereby indicating clearly that a period of reconciliation and political stability has returned.

---

30. Cooper (1970), *op. cit.*, p.156.

E. Cabinet changes to inject new untainted blood, remove targets of popular discontent.

F. Elections—These should be held, should be free, and should be widely observed.

G. Assembly—Assembly should be convoked soon after the elections. The Government should submit its policies to it and should receive its confidence. An assembly resolution would be most useful for external image purposes...[31]

Thus, U.S. pressure for political reform emphasized a more broadly based national government, improved civil liberties, and increased political restraint toward the opposition. The question of whether some more broadly based government might be less effective in satisfying popular desires was never squarely faced (for example, broadening representation to include small landlords might adversely affect land reform for the peasants). Proposition DM10 implied that opposition to Diem was based on the exclusivity of his government. Therefore, little was said about the nonmilitary aspects of government conduct in the countryside, the behavior of troops and officials, or policies concerning land tenure and corvees.

The combination of North Vietnamese sponsorship and the Diem government's narrowness made it easy for the decisionmakers to explain the insurgency. Even so, it seemed puzzling that a mere 15,000-20,000 insurgents could be creating such difficulties for the GVN. The additional explanatory factor was found in the perception that South Vietnam was a not very highly organized society, governed by a weak administrative apparatus that, according to Proposition DM8, could benefit greatly from American assistance.

---

31. White House (1963, September 17). Document #45: White House Cable to Lodge on Pressure for Saigon Reforms. In Sheehan et al. (1971), p. 206.

Aside from the morale factor, the Vietnamese Government is caught in interlocking circles of bad tactics and bad administrative arrangements which pin their forces on the defensive in ways which permit a relatively small Viet-Cong force (about one tenth the size of the GVN regulars) to create conditions of frustration and terror certain to lead to a political crisis, if a positive turning point is not soon achieved.[32]

Thus it was taken as natural that the GVN required relatively large doses of aid and resources compared with those being provided to the Viet Cong by the North. This requirement for aid was buttressed by the imputed input ratios for successful counterinsurgency, which were estimated from experience to be about 10 or 15 to one. The decisionmakers never carefully examined whether achieving this ratio was just sufficient to win with a functioning central government or was merely a threshold that had to be surpassed with a dysfunctional central government. The ratio was never adjusted according to any substantive grievances the population may have had against their government. Instead, attention was focused on achieving political representation as if this would guarantee that the 10 or 15 to one ratio would then be sufficient. If political representation were achieved, then the United States could provide the GVN the minimum additional assistance and forces so that an effective winning ratio could be achieved.

Poor military performance was attributed to bad intelligence, to bad organization, to bad training, all of which U.S. aid and training could cure (Proposition DM8). The lack of strategic and tactical intelligence, crucial in a guerrilla war, was attributed primarily to Viet Cong terror and coercion.

But the United States could supply better training, support and direction, better communications, transportation and intelligence,

---

32. Taylor, M. (1961, November 1). Document #2: Cablegram to President Kennedy. In Sheehan et al. (1971), p. 144.

better weapons, equipment and logistics—all of which the South
Vietnamese needed, said his advisers, if they were to reorient
their efforts to fight guerrilla battles.[33]

So it appeared natural rather than unfavorable that GVN personnel
needed extensive U.S. training to become proficient in countering
the Viet Cong, who needed no such equivalent training.

Two conclusions followed from this kind of assessment. First,
though policy reform was necessary, the military situation would
receive priority. Whether this was a correct decision or not, it at
least moved beyond the unspecified mix of instruments contained
in Proposition DM9. Second, little difficulty would be foreseen in
upgrading the organizational capabilities of the GVN (Proposition
DM8). Debate focuses on whether a *quid pro quo* would be or
could be exacted from the GVN leadership (Proposition DM11,
reform) or whether aid would be delivered untied (Proposition
DM11, Converse: But do not rock the boat).

For Asian politicians, pressure for results by putative external
allies such as the United States was counterproductive. They would
not undertake any short run military or political changes to
improve their counterinsurgency capabilities without an elaborate
and time consuming differential calculus of the impact of each
proposed action on their relative and absolute power. When
changes in power were purely theoretical, Asian politicians would
always tell their allies they were willing to act. So they held that
U.S. aid should be offered without ties. The United States should
wait patiently for the promised actions to be taken in the long run.

Although Kennedy wrote Diem in late 1961 that U.S. support
was contingent on reform, aid, in fact, was delivered without
reform. Nor did reform follow the aid. True reform meant a Diem
undertaking to remove himself and his family from power, an
unlikely course for any politician, East or West. The internal
security situation was serious and becoming worse. Thus, though

---

33. Sorenson, *op. cit.*, p. 654.

aid ostensibly depended on reform, it had to be granted unconditionally. As it had in the past, not rocking the boat (Proposition DM11 Converse) remained preferred to robust action to create an effective GVN (Proposition DM11).

In any case, reform and greater performance were incompatible. American criticism of GVN policies would decrease Diem's political stability. The more he was pressured for less one-man rule, the less he would be willing to depend on the United States making him even more reluctant to liberalize the regime. But the United States would see this reluctance as further reducing government performance. The United States simultaneously preferred not to rock the boat, but still believed it had the power to reform allies through its military assistance and the export of its own democratic forms of governance.

Another argument about the GVN was also involved. The United States considered GVN morale to have declined precipitously. No proposition in the model exists about how declines in allied morale came about, and no one argued that the decline appeared out of all proportion to its alleged causes. It seemed natural that U.S. policy in Laos, the buildup of the Viet Cong, and a flood in the Southern provinces could create a deep and pervasive crisis of confidence and a serious loss of national morale. But if this had occurred, then the United States would have to try to offset it.

If there were now no will to resist communist encroachment, it would have to be created (Proposition DM5) and it could be created by a set of limited actions (Proposition DM8, again).

The problem of defining limited action reached its most intense point within the U.S. government over the issue of troop commitments. The president decided not to commit combat troops but to prepare contingency plans for committing them. Schlesinger and Sorenson both cite President Kennedy as rejecting Proposition DM8, at least concerning the effects of troops:

> They say it's [U.S. troops] necessary in order to restore confidence and morale. But it will be just like Berlin. The troops will march in; the bands will play; the crowds will cheer; and in four

days everyone will have forgotten. Then we'll be told we will
have to send in more troops.[34]

But many believed that American troops were needed less for
their numerical strength than for the morale and will they could
provide to Diem's forces and for the warning they would provide
to the communists.

> Under present circumstances the problem of injecting United
> States and SEATO combat forces should, in large part, be
> considered as a contribution to the morale of the South Vietnam-
> ese in their own effort to do the principal job themselves.[35]

However, the president was unwilling to commit American
troops to fighting Asians on the Asian mainland for speculative
psychological reasons. It can be argued that the president did not
reject the Proposition DM8 idea of boosting an ally by the limited
use of U.S. power, but decided to test it. If the Vietnamese
succeeded with American aid, then a major infusion of combat
troops would not be necessary. If they did not, then the troop issue
could be taken up again (Proposition DM14, the incrementalism
that governed all U.S. policy). The president did order contingency
plans for United States intervention. Although there was some
doubt that American troops were appropriate for a low level
insurgency, there was little argument that they would be adequate
in larger contingencies. In the worst contingency, the entry of the
North Vietnamese Army into the war, the decisionmakers believed
200,000 troops would be sufficient. At this point, the decisionmakers believed that containing the insurgency remained a job for

---

34. Sorenson, *op. cit.*, p. 653. Sorenson goes ahead to speculate on
Asian psychological perceptions as the ground for Kennedy's rejection
of DM8.

35. Rusk, D. and McNamara, R. S. (1961, November 11).
Document #30: Report to President Kennedy. In Sheehan et al. (1971),
p. 151.

South Vietnam. Incremental commitments meant that it was always possible to defer any decision on large scale commitments of American troops.

THE LOGIC OF ESCALATION

Events since 1962 had been surprising to U.S decisionmakers. Although the United States had tried to change the GVN and had applied the nation-building propositions in its model, a competent ally had not yet emerged. The Viet Cong had adapted to the infusion of U.S. resources. North Vietnam had apparently read U.S. signals incorrectly or was not interested in reading them. The decisionmakers, however, did not interpret actual events as a challenge to the validity of their model. It had no built-in reflexive rules for evaluating or testing its own propositions. So they believed that the United States had not yet done enough to create GVN morale and to destroy Viet Cong morale and Northern will. However, doing ever more up to 1965 meant that the perceived United States commitment to maintaining the GVN would be strengthened (Proposition DM4 on expected future costs rising as U.S. effort increases).

By 1965 the Viet Cong had graduated from being just an insurgent movement. Viet Cong forces had moved to attacks on district towns and were closing in on provincial capitals. The decisionmakers now foresaw the imminent decline or end of the GVN.

> The security situation in the countryside has continued to deteriorate. The Viet Cong retain the initiative and are applying increasing pressure on a nationwide scale, from the northern coastal lowlands to the Camau peninsula. They have improved their firepower and capabilities for large operations and have increased daring and improved coordination and planning in their attacks, ambushes, and sabotage. They have strengthened their armed forces and military organization, in part, from increased infiltration, particularly in the northern provinces. Finally, Viet

Cong control is spreading over areas heretofore controlled by the
government, and the insurgent military presence is now closer
than ever before to an increasing number of urban centers, major
installations, and transportation lines.[36]

This condition left the decisionmakers with two choices. According to William Bundy,

To "muddle through" was almost certainly to "muddle out" and
to accept communist control of South Viet Nam, achieved by
force with outside support... [37]

There were, in short, only two choices: to move toward withdrawal, or to give a lot more help, both for its military impact and,
at the outset, to prevent a collapse of South Vietnamese morale and
will to continue. As deliberation continued within the administration, the matter was brought to a head by sharp attacks on U.S.
installations. These were serious provocations in themselves, but
above all they confirmed the decisionmakers' belief that North
Viet Nam was supremely confident, was moving in for the kill, and
would in fact succeed, perhaps in months.

The sunk costs of Proposition DM4 had clearly raised the
stakes to the level of major confrontation implied by Proposition
DM3. John McNaughton, a principal assistant to Secretary
McNamara provides an eloquent view of the escalation of the
struggle.

Evaluation: It is essential—however badly SEA may go over the
next 1-3 years—that United States emerge as a "good doctor."
We must have kept promises, been tough, taken risks, gotten
bloodied, and hurt the enemy very badly. We must avoid harmful

---

36. NSC Working Group on Vietnam. (1964, November 24).
Document #240: Intelligence Assessment of the Situation in Vietnam. In
Pentagon Papers (1971), vol. 3, p. 651.
    37. Bundy (1967), *op. cit.*, p. 658.

appearances which will affect judgments by, and provide pretexts to, other nations regarding how the United States will behave in future cases of particular interest to those nations—regarding United States policy, power, resolve and competence to deal with their problems. In this connection, the relevant audiences are the Communists (who must feel strong pressures), the South Vietnamese (whose morale must be buoyed), our allies (who must trust us as "underwriters") and the United States public (which must support our risk-taking with United States lives and prestige).[38]

McNaughton had certainly pinned down the symbolic and signaling character the struggle had now attained, given the costs the United States had already incurred. He does not present a similar estimate of the possible benefits and costs of cutting one's losses nor does he discuss what the signal content of such a strategy might be. The decisionmakers in other nations calculating their national interests might consider overinvestment in this struggle counterproductive to their needs for U.S. support.

Secretary McNamara was most clear about the meaning of the sunk costs.

> No matter how the struggle may have started, it has long since become one of the testing places between a free form of government and dictatorship.[39]

---

38. McNaughton, J. (1965, March 24). Document #96: Draft for Secretary McNamara. In Sheehan et al. (1971), p. 438.

39. McNamara, R. S. (1965, August 5). Statement before the Senate Subcommittee on Department of Defense Appropriations, excerpts published in *New York Times*.

And, on May 4, 1965, President Johnson said:

> Now make no mistake about it, the aim in Vietnam is not simply
> the conquest of the South, tragic as that would be. It is to show
> that the American commitment is worthless ... [40]

In 1965 there seemed no way to repress the combined Viet
Cong/NVA forces through more aid to the GVN. Maxwell Taylor,
now the U.S. ambassador to Vietnam reported as follows:

> As our programs plod along or mark time, we sense the mounting
> feeling of war weariness and hopelessness which pervade South
> Viet-Nam, particularly in the urban areas. Although the prov-
> inces for the most part appear steadfast, undoubtedly there is
> chronic discouragement there as well as in the cities. Although
> the military leaders have not talked recently with much convic-
> tion about the need for "marching North," assuredly many of
> them are convinced that some new and drastic action must be
> taken to reverse the present trends and to offer hope of ending
> the insurgency in some finite time.
>   The causes for the present unsatisfactory situation are not
> hard to find. It stems from two primary causes, both already
> mentioned above, the continued ineffectiveness of the central
> government, and the other, the increasing strength and effective-
> ness of the Viet-Cong and their ability to replace losses. [41]

Given this strengthened view of American commitment and
involvement in confrontations. There would clearly be "a lot more

------

40. Johnson, L. B. (1965, May 4). Remarks to Committee
Members on the Need for Additional Appropriations for Military
Purposes in Viet Nam and the Dominican Republic. *Public Papers of the
Presidents of the United States-Lyndon B. Johnson*, Vol. 1, item no.
227, p. 486.
41. Taylor, M. (1964, November 27).Document #87: Taylor's
Briefing of Key Officials in November '64. In Sheehan et al. (1971), p.
371.

help" rather than withdrawal. The sunk cost proposition implies that the costs of withdrawal will be weighted much higher than any costs of continuing.[42] Consequently the issue became what additional instruments could the United States apply that were (1) not really dependent on the performance of the indigenous ally, (2) would enhance the ally's will and morale, and (3) would give a clearer and stronger signal to the adversary.

BOMBING THE NORTH

Questions of coercing or punishing the North had occurred in 1961. As revealed by Taylor:

> Both of these courses of action [bombing of the North and U.S. troop commitments] had been under consideration at least since November 1961, when I presented my report to President Kennedy following a visit to Saigon to appraise the growing criticality of the situation.[43]

During 1962 the question of retaliation against the North was not urgent. Since limited aid appeared to be doing the job, the cautious incrementalism of Proposition DM14 governed. After President Kennedy's death in 1963, and after the continuing political deterioration following the overthrow of Diem, advocates of coercing the North through bombing were heard more frequently. The lack of success consequent upon the application of top-level organizational restructuring (Proposition DM11) strengthened the

---

42. George Ball, effectively the captive, show-off Dove of the administration did dissent strongly. Ball argued that the administration was exaggerating the short run costs of some compromise settlement and was underestimating the long-run costs of American forces bogged down in a war that could never be won. The long-run costs, according to Ball, would be "catastrophic." See Ball, G.W. (1965, July 1). Document # 103: A Compromise Solution in Vietnam. In Sheehan et al., p. 449.

43. Taylor (1966), p. 171.

case that the military proposition DM12, that the United States military establishment could put together a winning strategy, and Proposition DM13, that escalation could compel an adversary to act in a way preferred by the United States, should be used. The military were consistently strong advocates of direct action as was Walt Rostow.

The choice of the instrument of military escalation could be expected to have the following effects:

1. Boost sagging GVN morale (proposition DM8: United States resolve providing signals to an ally that it was not alone).

> We emphasize that our prime target in advocating a reprisal policy in the improvement of the situation in South Vietnam. Action against the North is usually urged as a means of affecting the will of Hanoi to direct and support the VC. We consider this an important but longer range purpose. The immediate and critical targets are in the South—in the minds of the South Vietnamese and in the minds of the Viet Cong cadres.[44]

2. Break the North's will to achieve victory (Proposition DM7: United States resolve providing signals to an adversary).

3. Impose increasing costs (Proposition DM13: Escalation brings enemy compliance because of damage suffered)

The initial choice of air power rather than ground escalation well illustrated another point in the decisionmakers' model—the incrementalism of proposition DM14. Air is clean and "surgical," can be put in and pulled out quickly, and, it was thought, could be based in sanctuaries on land or sea. The commitment of ground power seemed more permanent.

---

44. Bundy, M. (1965, February 7). Document #92: McGeorge Bundy Memo to Johnson on "Sustained Reprisal" Policy. In Sheehan et al. (1971), p. 425.

Most of the expected effects of air escalation appear in an interview with General Taylor in August 1965.

> There are three purposes duly announced, clearly thought through, before embarking upon this program. The first was to give the South Vietnamese people the sense of being able to strike back for the first time against the source of all their evil, namely, North Vietnam. And I can assure you the psychological effect, the morale effect of this decision was most visible throughout all of South Vietnam—military and civilians alike. The second ... to reduce not eliminate infiltration. We know air can't eliminate infiltration any more than it could in Korea. On the third point and perhaps most important in the long pull is to remind the leaders in Hanoi ... that unless they do not ease their aggression they're going to pay an increasing price to the point that the game is not worth this kind of loss....anyone who looks at the map and sees the destruction caused certainly would be convinced that this is having a vast impact.[45]

The interaction among all these effects would create greater leverage for the United States in conducting the war. The existence of multiple but untested reasons, however, suggests within-group disagreement among policymakers on which effects would predominate. The need to bolster the GVN has already been discussed. However, once the bombing of the North was decided, direct effects on the North and on the North's actions on the South began to dominate. Southern morale itself came to depend upon doing intensive damage to the North.

The substantive arguments about bombing were buttressed by emotional ones. The attack on Pleiku produced a very strong reaction in U.S. decisionmakers. McGeorge Bundy, on the scene at Pleiku shortly after the attack, gave an emotional report on the

---

45. CBS News Special Report. (1965, August 16). How Can We Win? Reprinted in *Congressional Record, Senate*, August 24, 1965. General Taylor repeated exactly these reasons in his February 1966 testimony before the Senate Foreign Relations Committee.

carnage. Weeks later, in his White House office, Bundy was still venting over the President's right and duty to protect American boys against being butchered in their tents (Wicker, 1968).

The attempted coup d'etat on February 19, 1965 convinced the decisionmakers that the GVN's morale was in decline. To arrest the decline, the United States would have to make the North pay more for its involvement through "offensive" rather than "defensive" or purely retaliatory strikes as it considered the Pleiku response to have been.

Discussion centered on the best way of achieving the desired effects on the North. The range of violence could extend from graduated reprisals to a dramatic show of power. The military had a long-standing belief that heavy damage in a short period would maximize psychological impact, but this was not tried; the more graduated escalation implied by Proposition DM13 was. The assumption of escalation in Proposition DM13 was that the North would be willing to support the Viet Cong only at low cost to itself and at low risk to the industrial complex around Hanoi. So even a small threat here would bring compliance. This issue about the means of inducing compliance in an adversary was to play a role in the 1967-1968 crisis of the model described in the next section.

The third effect hoped for from the bombing was reduction of North-to-South infiltration. Although it was controversial, the civilian decisionmakers accepted the military belief that bombing could reduce the infiltration sharply (Proposition DM12 and its corollary concerning proper organization for war). Critics argued that interdiction of the supply routes would simply raise Northern morale. Nevertheless, the administration saw the issue differently.

...The U.S. is prepared—at a time to be determined—to enter into a second phase program, in support of the GVN and RLG, of graduated military pressures directed systematically against the DRV. Such a program would consist principally of progressively more serious air strikes, of a weight and tempo adjusted to the situation as it develops (possibly running from two to six months). Targets in the DRV would start with infiltration targets south of the 19th parallel and work up to targets north of that point. This could eventually lead to such measures as air strikes on all major military-related targets, aerial mining of DRV ports, and a United States naval blockade of the DRV. The whole sequence of military actions would be designed to give the impression of a steady, deliberate approach, and to give the United States the option at any time (subject to enemy reaction) to proceed or not, to escalate or not, and to quicken the pace or not. Concurrently, the U.S. would be alert to any sign of yielding by Hanoi and would be prepared to explore negotiated solutions that attain United States objectives in an acceptable manner.[46]

On February 28, 1965, President Johnson ordered continuous limited air strikes against North Vietnam to reduce infiltration and force the North into negotiations.

In 1965 there was no way to test beliefs about escalation and bombing except to carry out the bombings. By April 1965, the decisionmakers had an initial evaluation of effectiveness from the CIA.

I have reported that the strikes to date have not caused a change in the North Vietnamese policy of directing the Viet Cong insurgency, infiltrating cadres, and supplying material. If anything, the strikes have to date hardened their attitude.[47]

Two years later the question of whether the beliefs had been given an adequate test would be debated intensely in public and private. The propositions in the decisionmakers' models are

---

46. Working Group (1964, November 29). Document #88: Draft Position Paper on Southeast Asia. In Sheehan et al. (1971), pp. 374-375.

47. McCone, J. A. (1965, April 2). Document #97: Memorandum on the Effectiveness of the Air War. In Sheehan et al. (1971), p. 440. McCone concluded that the bombing would have to be much heavier, but that public opinion in the United States and around the world would prevent it from becoming heavy enough. So ground troops would be needed. However, he doubted that these would be effective without increasing the weight of the strikes.

ambiguous with respect to the time required to realize predicted consequences, and this ambiguity left room for competing propositions about increasing the intensity of the war.

TROOPS

By the spring of 1965, it was apparent that bombing would not achieve all three of the objectives postulated and might achieve none. Viet Cong activity had intensified and the North Vietnamese did not respond to a short bombing pause in May. They appeared to be adapting to the bombing. The failure of the VC in the South would have to be shown.

What the bombing had done—unambiguously—was to raise the stakes by increasing sunk costs following Proposition DM4. Following the escalation logic of Proposition DM13, then, what was needed was a stronger signal. And this was found in the commitment of United States combat troops.

There was initially some debate about the particular military concept to be employed. Potential uses of the military widened from providing air base security to sustaining enclaves to a mobile search and destroy mission. On April 1, President Johnson approved an 18-20 thousand men increase in U.S forces and approved a change of mission for marine battalions in country.[48] The shifting rationale is documented by Generals Wheeler and Taylor in a television interview in August 1965.

Mr. Kalischer: General Wheeler: What is our grand strategy out there now as far as the employment of United States forces?

Gen. Wheeler: ...Now General Westmoreland has organized—and I think Da Nang is a fine example—has organized these in such a way that the forces as they come in are disposed

---

48. Bundy, M. (1965, April 6). Document #98: National Security Action Memorandum 328 to the Secretaries of State and Defense and the Director, CIA. In Sheehan et al. (1971), p. 442.

to protect these bases. This is the first charge against them. Afterwards, they begin to extend their area of influence out from the base area. As the forces have increased, he has started to use certain of his battalions to act in support of the Vietnamese for us who are actually out finding the enemy.

Mr. Kalischer: Don't we, sir, also sometimes airlift American troops to certain strategic areas far from these bases in order to shore up a situation that is getting out of hand?

General Wheeler: You are absolutely right ... that I do airlift these people into where the combat area is either occurring or is expected to occur so that they can furnish support at need.

General Taylor: Certainly I don't contemplate what I gather some people are talking about—sitting on the coast and sitting out this war. General Westmoreland expects to use his troops in the most advantageous way to bring this thing to a close....We are going to use our firepower and mobility to destroy, to assist in destroying the Viet Cong units: but the clearing, the holding, the bringing in of the governmental agencies ... that clearly is a Vietnamese function.[49]

The complements of this strategy were discussed by Admiral Sharp in a speech on August 12, 1965:

We are also using our air power with great effectiveness within South Vietnam in support of ground forces. If the Viet Cong move into large—scale engagements where they try to occupy land and stand and fight, these air operations will be even more important.

In recent weeks, special attention has been given to certain Viet Cong "war zones" in South Vietnam which the enemy has been

---

49. CBS News Special Report. (1965, August 16). Vietnam Perspectives: How Can We Win?

using as base areas for supplies, training and refuge. Therefore, high level bombing attacks have been launched against some of these isolated areas by B-52 bombers of the Strategic Air Command. These attacks have opened up areas which have long been communist strongholds and disrupted communist plans for attack.[50]

At this point the war had changed into an American war. American instruments for a solution existed, even if there were no Vietnamese ones. Because of the belief in Proposition DM12, it is an open question whether the decisionmakers realized that the force required could become unbounded. Although, objectively, United States troop requirements became a function of the VC/NVA response, the decisionmakers had little doubt that the United States had the resources. In several 1965 interviews concerning Vietnam, Secretary McNamara expressed confidence American resources would prevail, because he had provided large percentage increases in general purpose forces earlier in his tenure.

The predictions that the military made in exchange for the resources for the search and destroy mode are taken up in detail in Chapter 4. In short, the decisionmakers predicted that U.S. forces after several years would succeed in destroying the VC/NVA main forces permitting the RVNAF to destroy the local forces and the infrastructure.

In private, the decisionmakers were far less sanguine. McNamara now estimated that it would take more than the 312,000 troops to be deployed by the end of 1965.[51]

   ...We believe that, whether or not major new diplomatic initiatives are made, the U.S. must send a substantial number of

50. Sharp, U.S.G. (1965, August 12). Address before the Institute on World Affairs, San Diego, CA.

51. McNamara, R. S. (1965, November 30). Document #107: Memorandum for President Lyndon Johnson. In Sheehan et al. (1971), p. 489.

additional forces to VN if we are to avoid being defeated there. (30 Nov program; concurred in by JCS)...

Deployments of the kind we have recommended will not guarantee success. Our intelligence estimate is that the present Communist policy is to continue to prosecute the war vigorously in te South. They continue to believe that the war will be long one, that time is their ally, and that their own staying power is superior to ours. They recognize that the United States reinforcements of 1965 signify a determination to avoid defeat, and that more US. troops can be expected. Even though the Communists will continue to suffer heavily from GVN and U.S ground and air action, we expect them, upon learning of any U.S. intentions, to augment its forces. United States capabilities to boost their own commitment and to test US. capabilities and will to persevere at higher level of conflict and casualties.[52]

McNamara went on to worry about possible Chinese intervention if United States troop commitments were to rise to the 600, 000 level he now thought it would take to win. Tasking all factors into account:

It follows, therefore, that the odds are about even that, even with the recommended deployments, we will be faced in early 1967 with a military standoff at a much higher level, with pacification still stalled, and with any prospect of military success marred by the chances of an active Chinese intervention.[53]

THE MODEL IN CRISIS: SUMMER 1967 TO SPRING 1968

Toward the end of 1966, the decisionmakers themselves finally started questioning their model. There was doubt about the

---

52. McNamara, R. S. (1965, December 7). Document #108: Military and Political Actions Recommended for South Vietnam. In Sheehan et al. (1971), p. 489.

53. McNamara, R. S., *ibid.*, p. 490.

bombing; the validity of Proposition DM13 on escalation was questioned.

McNamara had come to believe that the pacification effort in the south and bombing in the north were both ineffective and would always be.

> Pacification is a bad disappointment. We have good grounds to be pleased by the recent elections, by Ky's 16 months in power, by the faint signs of development of national political institutions and of a legitimate civil government. But none of this has translated itself into political achievements at Province level or below. Pacification if anything has gone backward....
>
> Nor has the ROLLING THUNDER program of bombing the North either significantly affected infiltration or cracked the morale of Hanoi. There is agreement in the intelligence community on these facts....
>
> In essence, we find ourselves—from the point of view of the important war (for the complicity of the people)—no better, and if anything worse off. This important war must be fought and won by the Vietnamese themselves. We have known this from the beginning. But the discouraging truth is that, as was the case in 1961, 1963 and 1965, we have not found the formula, the catalyst, for training and inspiring them into effective action.[54]

In response to his own assessment, he recommended stabilizing the United States force into a permanent level of stalemate. Ground forces would have been leveled off at 470,000. He would have leveled off the number of sorties against the North, and would have established an electronic barrier to infiltration (the famous McNamara line).

McNamara's doubts had become known publicly by summer 1967. He told the Congress:

---

54. McNamara, R. S. (1966, October 14). Document #118: Draft Memorandum for President Lyndon B. Johnson, Actions Recommended for Vietnam. In Sheehan et al. (1971), p. 543.

There is no basis to believe that any bombing campaign short of one which had population as its target would by itself force Ho Chi Minh's regime into submission.

...I am convinced however that the final decision in this conflict will not come until we and our allies prove to North Vietnam she cannot win in the South.[55]

But there was doubt also about whether the issue could really be decided in the South, given the ground war strategy that the United States had chosen or evolved—doubt, in other words, on Proposition DM12 about the ability to create an appropriate strategy and force structure.[56] This doubt burst out in a major controversy over the large incremental troop requests and over widening of the war. And there was doubt whether the increased pacification effort would work or work in time, questioning Proposition DM11 on our ability to reorganize foreign societies.

Two related events forced this reexamination of the model— disenchanted public opinion and discontinuous troop requests. Although perceptions of public opinion on the war had not played a large part in the logic of intervention or escalation—there was no DM proposition concerning domestic reaction to the war—the growing and perhaps surprising public discontent and polarization implied the need for a very basic reexamination of the strategy the United States had been pursuing. A Louis Harris Poll in June 1967 reported that 42 percent of the population had assumed a moderate or extreme Dove position. Forty percent supported administration policy but wanted escalation to force negotiations, and 18 percent

---

55. McNamara, R. S. (1967, August 26). Statement to Senate Subcommittee. In *Air War Against North Vietnam*, part 4, p. 274.

56. Early in 1967 Secretary McNamara explained the strategy as consisting of "search and destroy operations," "clear and secure," "reserve reactions," and defense of government centers. See Statement of Robert S. McNamara Concerning the FY 1967 Supplemental for Southeast Asia on January 23, 1967.

wanted an all out military effort.[57] By contrast, after the escalation
in 1965, the Gallup polls had reported 57 percent approved the
president's handling of the war, and only 24 percent felt it was a
mistake to get involved. By late summer of 1967, those who felt it
was a mistake had increased to 47 percent. The fraction approving
the handling never again rose above 40 percent.[58] Non-random
sampling by the press also showed the same.

> The cooing of the doves and the crying of the hawks are louder
> now as more Americans begin to abandon indecision and settle
> on one side or the other in the fierce debate over Vietnam. There
> is mounting evidence that this polarization of opinion, if
> continued long enough, may cost President Johnson dearly in
> 1968.[59]

Second, the continually growing number of United States troops in
Vietnam did not reduce the military demands for still more troop
commitments. The Joint Chiefs continuously endorse the need for
more troops.

> The FY 1968 force for SVN is primarily needed to offset the
> enemy's increased posture in the vicinity of the DMZ and to
> improve the environment for Revolutionary Development in I
> and IV CTZ's. To achieve the secure environment for lasting
> progress in SV N, additional military forces must be provided in
> order to (1) destroy the enemy main force, (2) locate and destroy

---

57. Robinson and Solomon (1967), p. 67. A moderate Dove was
defined as a person who agreed with the administration policy but
wanted reduction in escalation to encourage negotiations. A radical Dove
was a person who wanted an unconditional halt to bombing and a withdrawal of American troops from South Vietnam.

58. *Ibid.*, p. 69.

59. From a *Wall Street Journal* news round up. (1967, May 15)
Placed in the *Congressional Record, Senate* by Senator Fulbright.

district and provincial guerilla a forces, and (3) provide security for the population..[60]

An increment of 45,000 to 50,000 was approved, but the civilian decisionmakers implied that there would never be a call-up of reserves and a partial mobilization. This was the point where the model had to be reconsidered. Constantly increasing military requests were inherent in the "attrition" or search and destroy strategy that had come to dominate the conduct of the war.[61] If the objective was pushing the combined NVA/VC forces below some threshold level, and if the NVA/VC were always able to respond by putting in enough new troops to stay above the threshold, that implied a relatively open commitment. Such NVA/VC response also implied that the Northern resources allowing such a response had to be attacked more severely. Consequently, a debate over intensified bombing and geographic expansion of the war occurred along with the debate over troop commitments and calling up the reserves. Neither Proposition DM12 on the military control of war strategy nor DM13 on escalation was beyond question any longer.

Much of the debate occurred because of diminishing prospects of early success or, as contemporary accounts put it, emerging stalemate. David Broder reported in July of 1967:

> Skepticism has become the dominant tone not only of the political community here but also of the inner circle of the Johnson Administration.... Within the top rank of the Pentagon,

---

60. Joint Chiefs of Staff. (1967, April 20). Document #124: JCSM-218-67. In Sheehan et al. (1971), p. 565.

61. Bundy, M. (1965, April 6). Document #98: National Security Action Memorandum 328 to the Secretaries of State and Defense and the Director, CIA. In Sheehan et al. (1971), p. 442.

the State Department and the White House disbelief in an early favorable outcome is almost universal.[62]

The president himself in early August quoted his January 1967 speech to the nation explaining:

For the end is not yet. I cannot promise that it will come this year—or come next year. Our adversary still believes, I think tonight, that he can go on fighting longer than we can and longer than we and our allies will be prepared to stand up and resist.[63]

The Tet offensive that began on January 31, 1968 deepened the skepticism and brought the questioning of the model to public attention. But as noted, that questioning had already begun six to eight months earlier. Tet provided a fairly unambiguous illustration of the deficiencies of the model. The bombing of the North had not prevented the resources with which the Tet offensive had been mounted from flowing South. The US/ARVN forces in the South had not been sufficient to prevent major operations by the VC/NVN.

Thus, if the adversary were to be denied his short-run capabilities, still more troops and more air would be needed. This additional commitment to the military doctrine of Proposition DM12 would have to be provided in the face of the increasingly clear failure of the proposition thus far.

The military indicated that an early deployment of 30,000 troops was required and that a total of 200,000 would be needed to

62. Broder, D. S. (1967, July 11). The White House Sceptics. *Washington Post*.

63. Johnson, L. B. (1967, August 3). *A Special Message to the Congress: The Fate of the Budget and the Economy*.

buttress our forces in Vietnam and to replenish the strategic reserve.[64]

The question now was whether such an increment could really make a difference. It was hard for the civilian decisionmakers to believe that it could.

Writing analytically, Alain Enthoven, a policy adviser for the war's later phase, and Wayne K. Smith have the following implicit comment on the request.

...the enemy's ability to sustain losses of 200,000 men per year was of critical importance to any United States strategy that called for defeating the enemy through a war of attrition.... But even in the first half of 1968 when the bloodshed of the enemy Tet and spring offensives shocked American and South Vietnamese alike, estimated enemy losses had never approached 200,000 per year. In other words, the VC/NVA forces appeared to have the manpower to sustain the war for years at the intense level of the first half of 1968, including launching major country-wide offensives such as Tet. The United States could not hope to win a war of attrition within any reasonable period of years, even when the enemy was willing to fight on a massive scale.[65]

The entire model was now called into doubt:

Officials themselves comment in private about widespread and deep changes in attitudes, a sense that a watershed had been reached and that its meaning is just now beginning to be understood....

---

64. Cooper, *op. cit.*, p. 390. Cooper is not clear on the implication of this request. Evidently 200,000 more troops would have to be sent to Vietnam, but they would have to be replaced by calling up the reserves.

65. Enthoven and Smith, *op. cit.*, p. 297. See also Enthoven (1967), May 4). Memorandum for Secretary of Defense: Force Levels and Enemy Attrition. In *Pentagon Papers,* vol. v., pp. 461-462.

> But at every level of Government there is a sense that conflict, if
> expanded further, can no longer be called a limited war.[66]

The doubt affected all the propositions and suggested that systemic
questions about United States foreign policy were in order.

Proposition DM1, that a gain for communism was a loss for the
United States, had been in doubt for a long time—at least since the
Sino-Soviet split had shown that world communism was not
monolithic.

Proposition DM2, the domino theory, was doubted as the
leaders of Thailand, for example, showed no inclination to turn
themselves into communists, despite U.S. difficulties in Vietnam.
Could the United States compensate for any domino tendencies
created by its difficulties in Vietnam or even a loss? Proposition
DM3, the U.S. stake in winning confrontations was eroded along
with belief in Propositions DM1 and DM2. Would Berlin really go
if the United States left Vietnam?

Proposition DM4, on sunk costs, was thrown into question as
the size of the past costs and the required magnitude of further
investment became clearer. Proposition DM5, on an absolute need
to defeat communist insurgencies, was derived from Propositions
1- 4, and disappeared with time. Proposition DM6, on successful
insurgencies needing a sanctuary, perhaps still held, but doing
something about that sanctuary appeared infinitely more difficult
than it had when the bombing began in 1965. Proposition DM7, on
U.S. ability to force compliance by an adversary in a reasonable
time span through signals of resolve, commitment, and staying
power was clearly failing.

Proposition DM8, on U.S. ability to bolster an ally, continued
to work. American support for the new constitutional government
of Vietnam did keep it going, and even maintained its stability—at
least relative to what had gone before. Its democratic character and

---

66. Smith, H. and Sheehan, N. (1968, March 10). *New York
Times*.

its popularity were strongly questioned in public, however. Proposition DM9, on the undefined balance of military and political efforts, which had been drifting toward the military for years, took a sudden turn to the political.

Proposition DM10, on the hierarchy of security first, political democracy next, and economic and social reform last, had begun to disappear earlier with the institution of the "new model" pacification program that tried, with some success, to combine security and reform. Proposition DM11, on the ability of reform at the top to trickle down, also disappeared with "new model" pacification. Proposition DM12, on the military establishment's ability to fight conventional wars and insurgency, disappeared.

Proposition DM13, on escalation, seemed archaic. It could no longer be taken seriously.

Proposition DM14 on incrementalism, perhaps most seriously, was thrown into serious question. Incrementalism in the application of instruments had gotten the United States into deep inconsistencies between its objectives and its means.

On March 12, 1968, Senator Eugene McCarthy received 40 percent of the vote in the New Hampshire Democratic primary. On March 18 and 19, President Johnson convened his informal advisory group consisting of prominent men now outside the government, but who had been frequently consulted on the war by the president.

> At each consultation before March they had been overwhelmingly in favor of prosecuting the war vigorously with more men and material, with intensified bombing of North Vietnam, with increased efforts to create a viable government in the South.[67]

After receiving a series of frank briefings on the Vietnam situation, the advisors recommended to the president that:

---

67. Loory, S. H. (1968, May 31). *Los Angeles Times*.

Continued escalation of the war intensified bombing of North Vietnam and increased American troop strength in the South— would do no good. Forget about seeking a battlefield solution to the problem and instead intensify efforts to seek a political solution at the negotiating table.[68]

The president was reportedly surprised at the conclusions of the informal advisory group and asked to hear some of the briefings. The president asked tough questions.[69] On March 31, 1968, President Johnson told the nation:

Tonight I have ordered aircraft and our naval vessels to make no attacks in North Vietnam, except in the area north of the Demilitarized Zone where the continuing enemy buildup directly threatens allied forward positions and where the movements of their troops and supplies are clearly related to that threat.

...I have concluded that I should not permit the Presidency to become involved in the partisan divisions that are developing in this political year....

Accordingly, I shall not seek and will not accept, the nomination of my party for another term as your President....[70]

Thus, the civilian decisionmakers decided to level off the commitment in the South and de-escalate in the North. It was a decision as significant as America's abandonment of isolationism thirty years earlier, showing a recognition of American limits for the first time. It marked an abandonment of the model of United States interests and of means of maintaining those interests that had evolved over thirty-five years.

---

68. *Ibid*.

69. *Ibid*.

70. Johnson, L. B. (1968, March 31). Remarks of the President to the Nation.

CHAPTER 4

THE MILITARY MODEL

Although the value propositions in the military model are nominally the same as those held by the civilian decisionmakers, there were strong differences in (1) how these values were to be maintained, and (2) the predicted outcomes from the military force that was being applied or that could be applied in the future. As the war went on, the Joint Chiefs of Staff (JCS) and the Secretary of Defense differed strongly, and unusually publicly, in both their factual assertions and predictions.

The military model is far better articulated with respect to the military inputs in conflicts than it is to political inputs. Tension arises between the decisionmakers' model and the military's model because of different beliefs about the purpose of war and the expected effectiveness of different strategies and tactics. Characteristically, the military model is open-ended with respect to the use of force. Sufficient force is to be applied sequentially until the enemy is defeated. Preferred strategies and tactics remain constant, and they fail only because decisionmakers do not authorize force on a large enough scale.

THE STRUCTURE OF THE MILITARY MODEL[1]

A. U.S. Values and Interests

The propositions concerning U.S. values and interests in the military model are identical to the five propositions found in the civilian decisionmakers' model set up and discussed in Chapter 3.

MM1. $\equiv$ DM1. *The conflict between communists and noncommunists is a conflict over the control of nation-states. A gain for the communists implies some loss for the United States.*

MM2. $\equiv$ DM2. Domino proposition: *The probability of additional communist gains rises after even a single gain.*

Alternative MM2. $\equiv$ DM2. Geographical domino proposition: *The probability of additional communist gains increases particularly strongly in countries near any one gained by the communists.*

MM3. $\equiv$ DM3. *The morale, confidence, and behavior of other nations in resisting communism rise and fall in response to U.S. efforts at resistance.*

When and if the United States does not resist, then other nations will become easier targets for communist adversaries or will allow the communists to gain control.

MM3.1. Corollary. *Confronting and resisting communism everywhere is itself a national interest.*

MM4. $\equiv$ DM4. Sunk costs: *The anticipated costs to the United States measured by the future calculations and behavior of allies and adversaries rises in proportion to the size of each previous effort. The expected domestic political costs of disengaging from an effort to resist rises in proportion to the size of each previous effort.*

---

1. We use *MM* to denote the propositions in the military model. The identity sign ($\equiv$) means that the propositions are the same.

MM5. ≡ DM5. *Whenever the United States forecasts that an ally is unable to contain or defeat communist insurgency, the United States must attempt to defeat it.*

B. How Insurgency Conflicts Work Politically

The military model uses the strong version of Proposition DM6 in the model for the civilian decision-makers:

MM6. ≡ DM6. *Unless external inputs to a communist insurgency are prevented from increasing, then even an effective ally and substantial commitment of United States forces will lead to stalemate.*

MM7. ≡ DM7. *An adversary will recognize the positive relation between U.S. resource inputs and increased U.S. will and commitment.*

Nation-building propositions MM8-MM9 are the same as that of the civilian decisionmakers.

C. How Insurgency Conflicts Work Militarily

MM10. *The volume of military resources applied directly to defeating or destroying an opposing force should be large enough to cover the worst possible response of the opposing force.*

MM11. *Military instruments are most effective in coercing or signaling an adversary when applied without pause and in great quantity.*

The Joint Chiefs always argued that not enough pressure had been exerted in a short enough time span.

The Joint Chiefs of Staff recognize that defining what might constitute appropriate counteroperations in advance is a most difficult task. We should therefore maintain our prompt readiness to execute a range of selected responses, tailored to the

developing circumstances and reflecting the principles in the
Gulf of Tonkin actions, that such counteroperations will result in
clear military disadvantage to the DRV. These responses,
therefore, must be greater than the provocation in degree, and not
necessarily limited to response in kind against similar targets.[2]

The civilian decisionmakers rejected military proposals to end
the war quickly and decisively by intense bombing of the North in
as short a time as possible. The signal content of the bombing was
more important than the damage. According to Secretary of Defense McNamara, thirty years later, each side was trying to signal
the other about its limited intentions. However, the bombing
eventually persuaded the North Vietnamese that the United States
would settle for no less than unconditional surrender. The Northern
escalation of the war in the South as both a feasible and cost-
effective response to the bombing showed the United States that
the North would settle for no less than unconditional surrender.

MM12. *If a civilian commitment to war is made, and if the
military makes decisionmakers aware of the possible military
responses of the adversary, then the military should be provided
with the volume of resources required to meet each response and
should determine the allocation of these resources.*
     MM12.1. *Major field commanders should have a major voice
in setting force levels.*
     MM12.2. *Major field commanders should always have
operational control of forces.*

MM12, MM12.1 and MM 12.2 are central to nearly all of the
controversies between the military and the civilian decisionmakers.
Propositions MM12.1 and MM12.2 were never accepted by U.S.
civilian decisionmakers. To them, military operations were

---

2. Joint Chiefs of Staff. (1964, August 26). Document #78:
Recommended Courses of Action-Southeast Asia. In Sheehan et al.
(1971), p. 355.

signaling devices, and they were going to try to control the signal content, its magnitude, and its timing. In contrast, the military believed in the "total war" thinking and experience that nearly all senior military officers had gained in World War II.

MM13. *The U.S. military establishment had evolved or could easily evolve an effective strategy and force structure for conducting military operations in conventional and insurgent environments and for controlling the signal content of those operations.*
MM13.1. *The military objective is destruction of the enemy's forces (rather than, for example, capture of territory).*
MM13.2. *In guerrilla warfare, destruction translates to attrition; there is a negative relation between attrition and the adversary's will and ability to continue a conflict.*[3]

This argument appeared in public in the 1967 *Hearings Concerning the Air War Against North Vietnam.* Taking the strategic offensive is an effective way to attrite an adversary, especially given superior mobility and firepower and a larger volume of resources.

MM13.3. *The strategic offensive should be carried out by rigorously trained troops.*
MM13.4. *Forces lacking training, mobility, and firepower can be used effectively for area control, for population control, and in attempts to win popular support.*
MM13.5. Conclusion: *American forces will necessarily have the dominant role in carrying out an attrition strategy.*
MM14. *Air interdiction is powerful enough to substantially decrease the flow of personnel and logistics support from a supporting communist nation.*

---

3. See McNamara, Blight, and Brigham (1999), pp. 213, 271, 303-304.

MM14.1. *A negative relation exists between the quantity and intensity of air power applied to a communist nation supporting an insurgency and the casualties suffered by United States and allied forces.*

D. How Policy is Made

MM15. *Within the constraints imposed by civilian decision-makers, military plans and operations should be ranked according to their expected military effectiveness. The most effective should be chosen without regard to how "incremental" they are.*

A RECOMMENDED LOGIC OF INTERVENTION, 1961

As early as spring 1961, the JCS had begun recommending a U.S. troop commitment in Vietnam. For example, General Lemnitzer, then Chairman of the Joint Chiefs, said in 1961:

> ...whatever aid was needed should be provided. If we don't do it [provide whatever aid is needed] we're going to lose these countries and see them dragged behind the Iron Curtain, and this is an unacceptable alternative.[4]

> 2. In view of the foregoing, the Joint Chiefs of Staff recommend that the decision be made now to deploy suitable United States forces to South Vietnam. Sufficient forces should be deployed to accomplish the following purposes:
> a. Provide a visible deterrent to potential North Vietnam and/or Chinese Communist action;

---

4. Belair, F. (1961, June 9). Seek More Authority to Help Nations Fight off Reds. *The New York Times*.

    b. Release Vietnamese forces from advanced and static defense positions to permit their fuller commitment to counterinsurgency;

    c. Assist in training the Vietnamese forces to the maximum extent possible consistent with their mission;

    d. Provide a nucleus for the support any additional United States and SEATO operation in Southeast Asia; and

    e. indicate the firmness of our intent to all Asian nations.[5]

However, achieving these things in the face of enemy opposition should it develop carried tacit derivative requirements for even more United States troops. As General Taylor put it:

> The U.S. action proposed in this report—involving as it does the overt lifting of the MAAG ceiling, substantial encadrement, and the introduction of limited United States forces— requires that the United States also prepare for contingencies that might arise from the enemy's reaction. The initiative proposed here should not be undertaken unless we are prepared to deal with any escalation the communists might choose to impose....
>
> In our view, nothing is more calculated to sober the enemy and to discourage escalation in the face of the limited initiatives proposed here than the knowledge that the United States has prepared itself soundly to deal with aggression in Southeast Asia at any level.[6]

The logical basis and psychological basis for these recommendations would be the decisionmakers' own propositions DM7 and DM8 that a sufficiently large demonstration of U.S. resolve would deter the enemy and strengthen the GVN. On the military side, U.S. combat units, although far more costly to operate than ARVN

    5. JCS. (1961, May 10). Document #19: Memorandum to Secretary of Defense: United States Forces in South Vietnam. In Sheehan et al. (1971), pp. 125-126.

    6. Taylor, M., Gen. (1961, November 3). Document #28. Taylor Report on Vietnam. In Sheehan et al. (1971), pp. 147-148.

units, would provide a more efficient substitute for ARVN forces in a combat role (Proposition DM13.5). The in-country presence of combat units would give the United States greater resources for upgrading ARVN capabilities.

Behind this action recommendation lay the value judgment that whatever steps were necessary to defend Southeast Asia should be taken (Proposition MM5). The military had combined proposition MM10 on preparing for the worst possible contingency, proposition MM12 on the civilians providing the military any needed resources once the decision to fight had been made, and proposition MM15 on the military choosing the war fighting options within broad civilian constraints. Consequently, there could never be an internal military calculation of the benefits to be gained and costs incurred from applying MM5.

Later in the year, when Taylor and Rostow made their recommendations for using U.S. troops, the military presumably supported the recommendation on the same grounds.

> We are of the opinion that failure [to deploy United States forces]... will merely extend the date when such action must be taken and will make our ultimate task proportionately more difficult.[7]

General Taylor had provided an upper bound in the worst contingency, a conventional attack from the North, about 205,000 U.S. troops would be needed. Whether this forecast served as a shock to the civilian policymakers or a reassurance is not clear. In Laos the decisionmakers had already been "shocked" by a request for preauthorized use of nuclear weapons.[8]

---

7. JCS. (1962, January 27). Document #31: Memorandum to Secretary of Defense McNamara. In Sheehan et al. (1971), p. 155. The JCS requested that their memo be transmitted to the President, and it was.

8. See Ellsberg (1970) and Schlesinger (1967) for different perspectives on the alleged "shock."

In terms of the military model, the accepted Taylor-Rostow recommendation for an initial 8,000 troops implied a desire for a far greater commitment. The initially small contingent would not by itself stop the insurgency nor would it have been sufficient to generate signals of potential coercion if required. To be effective as signals, military actions must be large and continuous (MM11). The small scale use of military instruments in the coercive role gives an adversary the time and resources required for adaptation, making the original attempt ineffective.

One retrospective comment on the soundness of MM11 is worthy of note. The following exchange occurred between Dean Rusk and Henry Graff in 1967:

> I asked Rusk as I had asked McNamara: "Mr. Secretary, are there some things with respect to Vietnam in the last five years that you wish you had done differently?" He answered without hesitating that after the Vienna meeting of June 1961 we should have put down "a lot of blue chips immediately" to head off "misunderstanding by the other side,"and to make crystal clear: "you can't have South Vietnam.... Things would have turned out better if there had been more, sooner, rather than less."[9]

A MILITARY LOGIC OF ESCALATION FOR 1965

The military model implies that each "dose" of resources acquired from the civilian decisionmakers must be applied to the maximum extent possible (worst case MM10 and effective signals MM11). Decentralized resource allocation is necessary and appropriate during the conduct of war. MM12 demands resource allocation be decentralized to the top military command and then to field commanders by MM12.1. Some tension between the basic civilian model and the military model was bound to arise in 1965.

---

9. Graff (1970), pp. 87-88.

The decisionmakers' fear of war with China led them to insist on some control over the bombing of the North. The decisionmakers believed that they were sending clear signals to Hanoi by limiting the actual damage inflicted, but implying through those limits that even worse damage would come to the North if it did not stop its support of the Viet Cong in the South. However, there was far less conflict about the use and control of ground forces in the South until a few years later.

BOMBING

The military recommended a program of continuing, intense, sustained air attacks. The JCS believed this use of air power would be effective in forcing the enemy to stop its activities in the South and would eventually force him to the negotiating table (proposition MM11, maximum force is the most cost-effective signal available). In other words, compliance with U.S. preferences would be induced by creating ever heavier damage with no pauses and implying more to come. The military believed that any response by the enemy's allies or the allies of the United States would be manageable, if resources were provided (MM12—military requirements should be met).

The civilian decisionmakers had begun the bombing primarily as a strategy of graduated reprisal and signaling. After a few months, however, there was little evidence that the adversary was being impressed by the punctuated use of the U.S. potential to do him harm, and the competing propositions in the military model received some support. The following exchange between Senator Thurmond and General Wheeler, Chairman, JCS, is typical.

> Senator Thurmond: General Wheeler, the air war against North Vietnam has been categorized as a concept of gradualism because of the way it gradually moved from the southern part of North Vietnam northward to the northeast quadrant. Have the Joint Chiefs of Staff in any of their deliberations or position papers ever supported this gradualistic approach to waging war?

General Wheeler: We supported a much sharper type of attack, Senator Thurmond, than the concept that was adopted.

Senator Thurmond : How sharp an attack?

General Wheeler: For example, going back a long time —and this was at the time when we were talking of the 94-target list—I believe it was we advocated the strike of some, I think it was, 60 or 70 targets—no, I guess it was 90 targets—in about 16 strike days.The weather being what it was at that time, it would have come down to probably a span of some 26 days. And, of course, this is hindsight, because we can now look back at what the weather was. So this is what I mean by a sharper type of attack.[10]

These conflicts about the best way to coerce an adversary were not resolved in 1965 or even in 1967. Rather, military events during 1965 demanded a shift from beliefs about the psychological effects of bombing to beliefs in its direct military effects in reducing infiltration (a shift from MM11 to MM14 on air interdiction). Yet shifting from MM11 concerning the coercive use of military instruments to MM14 concerning direct military effects of an instrument does not mean MM11 would be abandoned or invalidated. There was no clear test for proposition MM11. So it would always provide a basis for proposals to extend the bombing and explain why bombing was never effective enough, no matter how much was done.

In the spring of 1965, the military began a test of its proposition MM14—that air power could sufficiently disrupt the adversary's lines of communication and war making capability up to the point where the rate of attrition in the South would forever rise above and stay above the rate of infiltration from the North. If this

---

10. Wheeler, E., Gen. (1967). Testimony. In U.S. Senate Armed Service Committee (1976). The 94-target list may be found in the testimony of other military principals.

situation could be achieved, then an attrition or "search and destroy" strategy on the ground in the South would eventually break the adversary's morale and will (MM13.1 on attrition).

TROOPS

By the middle of April 1965, bombing by itself was clearly not going to be sufficient. The United States would have to defeat the North Vietnamese and Viet Cong forces in the South, and so it would have to commit more troops. Recommendations for use of U.S. forces would quickly center on taking the war to the enemy. By Propositions MM13, MM13.1-MM13.5, comparative advantage lay in rapid attrition that could be attained by well-trained United States troops on the offensive. Although there were some early competitors, by the summer of 1965, what became known as the "search and destroy" strategy, was well on its way to becoming the strategy that would dominate the war and U.S. resource allocation until it came into question in 1967.

The rationale behind the search and destroy strategy was simple. The size, mobility, and firepower of U.S. general purpose forces had all been increased during the Kennedy-Johnson period. In any actual war, those forces would have some initial learning to do about the environment, but that period was expected to be quite short.

By comparison, GVN forces had much less mobility and fire-power than U.S. forces, let alone the organizational capability and will to engage in the necessary search and destroy. Over time, en-dowing GVN forces with these capabilities would have been possible so that they could conduct search and destroy missions. However, its current comparative advantage lay in operating in the populated areas. At least in theory, the ARVN had superior know-ledge of the population (Proposition MM13.4) compared with U.S. troops. Without the added American field capability, the actual fighting force ratios would become ever more adverse because of NVA infiltration and increasingly successful VC recruitment. In the short run, U.S. forces would have to supply the "search and destroy" capability that MACV and General Westmoreland wanted.[11]

In June 1965, General Westmoreland received the president's permission to commit U.S. ground forces anywhere in South Vietnam in support of RVNAF. At this point the basic military question became what force level would be required to defeat the adversary in the South. Although the adversary could respond to the search and destroy strategy, the United States could control any response by raising the costs of infiltration and resupply to high levels (Proposition MM14 on interdiction). If the VC/NVA main force were destroyed, then RVNAF could tackle the VC local forces and the guerrillas plus the VC infrastructure (Proposition MM13.4). The search and destroy strategy itself would control responses in the South.

The military forecast the following from a sustained bombing program in the North combined now with a search and destroy strategy in the South: In 1965 U.S. forces would learn the environment and blunt the adversary's offensive. In 1966-1967, these forces would seize the initiative. By 1968 the adversary's military capabilities would be so reduced that the GVN would be secure (Proposition MM9). Seeing this, the adversary would choose a "reasonable" negotiating posture.

> The first phase involved arresting the losing trend, stifling the enemy initiative, protecting the deployment of our forces, and providing security to populated areas to the extent possible. I

---

11. It is always possible to invent an *ex post* Occam's razor for each set of actors. For example, the decisionmakers wanted to stay in office by showing they could handle the communist challenge. A frequently presented alternative to the derivation of the search and destroy strategy constructed here is the very simple idea that the military had new and unused capabilities and so wanted to use them. However, the so-called "military mind" then or now is nowhere near that simple. Military models, like those of other actors, derive from a view of national interests and a set of ideas on how best to maintain them.

estimated that this phase would carry through to the end of 1965. In the second phase, United States and allied forces would mount major offensive actions to seize the initiative in order to destroy both the guerrilla and organized enemy forces, thus improving the security of the population. This phase would be concluded when the enemy had been warn down, thrown on the defensive, and driven well back from the major populated areas. The third phase would involve the final destruction of the enemy's guerrilla structure and main force units remaining in remote base areas.[12]

THE MILITARY STRATEGY IN CRISIS: SUMMER 1967 TO SPRING 1968

In March 1967, Army General Harold K. Johnson, evaluated the U.S. strategy and found it was working, if slowly.

I think that what is happening is much like cracking a walnut or a Brazil nut with a hammer. The enemy has been hit sharply everywhere and every time that he has been found, to the extent that he is fractured ... broken, like the half of a walnut but with a hammer into pieces. He tries to come back together but the free world has sufficient force now so that the pressure stays on, and he just cannot put this structure of his together.

It is a combination on our part of an enormous mobility differential, coupled with a determination to hit him-hard-each and every time....

...as we fracture the large units—crack the walnut —and as we bring pressure to bear on these middle units, there is going to be a withering of the terrorists.[13]

---

12. Westmoreland, W. C., Gen. (1968), p. 100.
13. Johnson, H. K., Gen. (1967, March 21). Vietnam Assessment—End 1966. Speech to Kansas City Chamber of Commerce, Kansas City, KS. This is a rather precise statement on the need for maximum force.

All this was in accord with attrition-offensive proposition MM13. Nevertheless, the military now foresaw a long war whose end depended upon reassessments induced in the adversary.

> The U. S. Commander in Vietnam said in an interview that his battle plan remains the same: We'll just go on bleeding them until Hanoi wakes up to the fact that they have bled their country to the point of natural disaster for several generations. Then they will have to reassess their position.
>
> My strategy is to put the pressure on the enemy everywhere and that includes the major bombing campaign in the North. The only way I know how to fight a war is by putting the maximum pressure on the maximum amount of time ... it is impossible to say how long the war will last, he said. I can't see any end in sight.[14]

Late in 1967 General Westmoreland added a fourth phase of the war that involved the United States in a more supporting role. He was now forecasting the war would definitely continue beyond 1968.

> I envisioned 1968 to be the year of the third phase in which we would continue to help strengthen the Vietnamese Armed Forces —turning over more of the war effort to increasingly capable and better armed forces. In the fourth—and decisive—phase I could see the United States presence becoming superfluous as infiltration slowed, the communist infrastructure was cut up and a stable government and capable Vietnamese Armed Forces carried their own war to a successful conclusion.[15]

Pursuing this strategy, by the end of 1966, the number of American troops stood at 389,000 with 54,000 third country forces, from Australia, South Korea, etc. GVN forces totaled about

---

14. Wheeler, J. (1967, April 14). Strategy of Westmoreland: Bleed Hanoi Till it Quits. *Washington Evening Star.*

15. Westmoreland, *op.cit.*, p. 136.

600,000 and the total VC/NVA forces according to Secretary
McNamara stood at 275,000 including 45,000 North Vietnamese
regulars, a gain of 25,000. North Vietnamese regulars had doubled
their strength.[16]
   A successful search and destroy strategy depended critically on
keeping the rate of infiltration down and on maintaining the proper
force ratio between United States forces and the VC/NVA forces.
The ARVN did not enter computations of the critical force ratio,
since only United States troops were effective in search and
destroy operations (MM13.5). Yet apparently the adversary
remained able to respond and did. In October 1966, Secretary
McNamara's assessment was:

> The one thing going for us in Vietnam over the past year has
> been the large number of enemy killed-in-action resulting from
> the big military operations. Allowing for possible exaggeration
> in reports, the enemy must be taking losses—deaths in and after
> battle—at the rate of more than 60,000 a year. The infiltration
> routes would seem to be one-way trails to death for the North
> Vietnamese. Yet there is no sign of an impending break in enemy
> morale and it appears that he can more than replace his losses by
> infiltration from North Vietnam and recruitment in South
> Vietman.[17]

Despite reportedly heavy attrition, a force ratio favoring the United
States and its external allies could not be achieved.
   By this time, the constant demands from the civilian decision-
makers and the highest ranking military for proof that the war was
being won had begun to corrupt the intelligence they were getting.
Since the conflict was not being fought for control of terrain, valid

   16. McNamara, R. S. (1967). In U.S. Congress House Committee
on Armed Services, p. 58.
   17. McNamara, R. S. (1966, October 14). Document #118:
Actions Recommended for Vietnam. In Sheehan et al. (1971), pp. 542-
543.

and reliable indicators of success were hard to come by. Body counts for the VC/NVA forces suffered from hyperinflation, as did estimates of the hamlets controlled by the United States and ARVN forces.

In March of 1967 General Westmoreland, as described earlier, requested an incremental 70,000 troops beyond the 470,000 approved for the end of that year. Actually, he said his optimum requirement was five more divisions, about 150,000 men, even though this "optimum" varied passively in relation to the NVA's infiltration rate. So this optimum could not really be specified without knowing the rate of NVA infiltration and its stability. Given that his optimum was unattainable, the general argued for honoring a minimum requirement of two more divisions with supporting units, about 70,000 men.[18]

This minimum request met with disturbing resistance from the perspective of military model. Military leaders maintained their beliefs in the basic value propositions MM1-MM5, concerning U.S. interests that the policymakers themselves had defined. Propositions MM10 through MM16 laid out a combined strategy that policymakers had until now supported. If the strategy were correct, and had been supported with resources authorized by the civilian decisionmakers, then the failure to bring the adversary to the bargaining table must be due to failure to apply yet enough resources. Therefore, the troop request should have appeared natural to the decisionmakers (MM12). Either they were shifting their view of U.S. values, or they had come to doubt the effectiveness of the U.S. strategy. But indirectly the latter implied a possible shift in all the original beliefs concerning U.S. interests. For if it were not feasible to defeat the adversary and create a viable GVN, then the United States might have to settle for denying victory to the adversary, rather than winning a victory itself. Only a United States victory would have maintained

---

18. Sheehan, Neil (1967, July 3). Joint Chiefs Back Troop Rise Asked by Westmoreland, *The New York Times*.

Propositions MM1-MM5, and the United States was not winning. Consistent with the decisionmakers' standard incremental response to any request, the 1967 debate about troop levels was resolved by adding 55,000 to the forces authorized for Vietnam and by not calling up the reserves.

The 1968 Tet offensive raised the whole issue again to new heights. Although General Westmoreland said the offensive had been expected, its size and power were unexpected. This time, two hundred thousand more men would be required.

> Forces currently assigned to MACV, plus the residual Program Five forces yet to be delivered, are inadequate in numbers to carry out the strategy and to accomplish the tasks described above in the proper priority. To contend with, and defeat, the new enemy threat, MACV has stated requirements for forces over the 525,000 ceiling imposed by Program Five. The add-on requested totals 206,756 spaces for a new proposed ceiling of 731,756, with all forces being deployed into country by the end of CY 68. Principal forces included in the add-on are three division equivalents, 15 tactical fighter squadrons and augmentation for current Navy programs.[19]

Despite the heavy attrition inflicted during Tet, the United States would still have to call up its reserves and would have to place the country on a semi-war footing. Although the question of 150,000-200,000 more men had first been raised in 1967, the shock of Tet provided a clear test for both the civilian and the military model. Secretary of Defense Clifford chaired the high level review of the troop request. This review now involved examination of the U.S. balance of payments and the need for price and wage controls. But the key issue was whether the last requested increment would be sufficient.

---

19. Wheeler, E. C. (1968, February 27). Document #132: Report of Chairman, JCS on Situation in Vietnam and MACV Requirements. In Sheehan et al. (1971), p. 620.

Clifford pressed the military on whether the additional troops would make the difference between victory and stalemate. The Joint Chiefs of Staff were unable to assure him that it would.[20]

No feasible volume of resources seemed large enough to counter a Northern response that would negate the value of the increment. Although it might have been true that U.S. forces had a comparative advantage in the strategic offensive and could inflict heavy attrition, it was now argued that the adversary always had the option of *not* fighting if he pleased. According to Enthoven and Smith:

> Correlation between enemy attacks and enemy losses were very high; similar correlations between friendly force activity and enemy losses were close to zero.[21]

In a memorandum to Secretary of Defense Clifford, Enthoven wrote:

> One important fact about the war in Vietnam is that the enemy can control his casualty rate, at least to a great extent, by controlling the number, size and intensity of combat engagements. If he so chooses, he can limit his casualties to a rate that he is able to bear indefinitely. Therefore, the notion that we can win this war by driving the VC/NVA from the country or by inflicting an unacceptable rate of casualties on them is false.[22]

Such analytical arguments counted little in policy making deliberations. They collided head on with worst case proposition MM10, attrition offensive proposition MM13, and air interdiction proposition MM14. After an intense debate over the option offered by the military and lesser options offered by the civilians, a

---

20. Cooper, *op. cit.*, p. 392.
21. Enthoven and Smith, *op. cit.*, p. 297.
22. *Ibid.* p. 298.

minimum increment of 13,500 men was authorized, indicating an intent to stabilize the war and to change United States' interests.

The crisis in the ground force search and destroy strategy described above was never articulated as clearly in public as the crisis of the bombing strategy. Congressional hearings showed more concern with the air war against the North than the ground war. The efficient and effective conduct of a ground war in an allied nation was being left to the military, but bombing the North always had international political implications. Nonetheless, there were now public complaints that the civilians were deciding too many targets in the North.

The 1967 air war hearings show the military upholding the efficacy of bombing and Secretary McNamara denying this efficacy, at least in part. According to the military, the bombing, after two years, was raising costs to the adversary and inflicting punishment. It was not sending signals that would bring the North to the bargaining table to offer an outcome preferred by the United States. A shift from arguing the coercive potential of bombing the North to its effects in the South had occurred by summer 1965. General Wheeler reported:

> During the past year, the air campaign has made an essential contribution to the war in Southeast Asia by forcing the enemy to mobilize; to divert large quantities of manpower and resources to maintain lines of communication and to man an extensive air and coastal defense system. Furthermore, during this period, North Vietnam has experienced a steady destruction of the country's physical infrastructure and deterioration of the national economy.[23]

He went on to recommend uninterrupted bombing, linking any reduction in bombing with increased U.S. casualties (proposition MM14). Reallocating aircraft to direct interdiction rather than

---

23. Wheeler, E., Gen. Testimony, *Air War Against North Vietnam*, p. 125. Admiral Sharp made the same response to this issue.

punishment, the JCS argued, would not buy major decreases in casualties, since this effort was already at a high level. Concerning proposals to restrict the bombing to south of 20° north latitude, General Wheeler was very specific. In 1967

> ...the Joint Chiefs of Staff examined the situation and we concluded that the concept was erroneous. In other words, there is a substantial target system remaining in the North or which is being rebuilt in the North and therefore there would be no advantage accruing by the thought of concentrating our air efforts against the Panhandle area of North Vietnam lying south of 20° north latitude.

> ...In my judgment this proposal is dead.[24]

General Wheeler went on to argue that allocation of air and naval resources to interdiction targets at an earlier part of the logistics pipeline was a way to get high payoff even though all supplies could not be cut off. Such action would raise costs significantly to the adversary.

> Mr. Kendall: With respect to Haiphong, I realize that political and policy matters are involved, but would I be correct in assuming that the closure or neutralization of Haiphong would be one of the most important things to do in North Vietnam at this time?

> General Wheeler: Yes.

> Mr. Kendall: Militarily?

> General Wheeler: Yes, militarily, the answer to that is yes.[25]

---

24. *Ibid.*, p. 133.
25. *Ibid.*, p. 161.

Admiral Sharp in his testimony argued in much the same manner as General Wheeler. The level of infiltration had been reduced (MM14). The resources that the North would have to devote to the war had been increased. Admiral Sharp argued that the costs to the North would have been higher and U.S. costs lower without the adopted tactic of graduated escalation.

> Repair, reconstruction, and dispersal programs are assuming increasing human and material resources which otherwise would contribute to the Communists' combat capability in South Vietnam. We believe about 500,000 men have been diverted to such activities.[26]

No Senator asked Admiral Sharp whether the diversion of 500,000 men represented a true opportunity cost. That is, were they employed resources or did they represent the surplus labor usually found in agricultural economies? Such a question would have been a direct test of this question.

> Mr. Kendall: Would it not have been better to have mounted an extensive and sustained air campaign against the more vital targets and kept it up from the south rather than have this incremental and graduated progression from a military standpoint?

> Admiral Sharp: Militarily, one of the things we seek is surprise and an impact on the enemy, and the way to do that, of course, is to, the first time you hit them, hit them with enough to do the maximum amount of damage, so I think the answer to the question is "Yes."

> Mr. Kendall: Would it follow from this slowly graduated bombing effort starting from a relatively few sorties against a limited number of targets in South Vietnam, and progressing to

---

26. Sharp, U.S.G., Adm., Testimony, *Air War Against North Vietnam*, Part I, p. 6.

the north, including more targets, gave the North Vietnamese time to prepare their defenses and thereby made the major targets more costly to us when we hit them belatedly.

Admiral Sharp: Yes, that is true, also gave them a chance to adjust for the campaign.[27]

As noted, the propositions contained in policy models do not vanish. Here we find Proposition MM11, the need for continuous large military applications plus the implication that more desirable outcomes would have occurred if the proposition had been employed by the civilians. Admiral Sharp went on to argue that coercion could still be achieved by inflicting more punishment now.

During the last 3 months, with an expanded target list but no significant departure from the broad restraints under which we have long operated, we have begun to hurt the enemy in his home territory. He is suffering painful military, economic, and psychological strains. Now, when the enemy is hurting, we should increase our pressures. The best way to persuade the ruling element in North Vietnam to stop the aggression is to counter that aggression in both North and South Vietnam to make the consequences of not stopping readily and painfully apparent.[28]

After very similar testimony by Air Force Chief of Staff General McConnell, and Chief of Naval Operations Admiral Moorer, Secretary McNamara testified on August 25, 1967. He agreed with the military that the bombing campaign had imposed costs on the North and reduced its war making capabilities. But he denied that the bombing could cut off increased supplies in the South or break the will of the North.

---

27. *Ibid.*, p. 40.
28. *Ibid.*, p. 8.

As to breaking their will, I have seen no evidence in any of the many intelligence reports that would lead me to believe that a less selective bombing campaign would change the resolve of the North Vietnamese leaders or deprive them of the support of the North Vietnamese people....

The course of conflict on the ground in the South, rather than the scale of air attack in the North may be the determining factor in North Vietnam's willingness to continue.[29]

On reducing infiltration and logistic flows, the Secretary commented:

But the capacity of the lines of communication and of the outside sources of supply so far exceeds the minimal flow necessary to support the present level of North Vietnamese military effort in South Vietnam that the enemy operations in the south cannot, on the basis of any reports I have seen, be stopped by air bombardment—short, that is, of the virtual annihilation of North Vietnam and its people. As General Wheeler has observed, no one has proposed such indiscriminate bombing of populated areas.[30]

And on closing of sea and land routes:

But far less than the present volume of imports would provide the essentials for continued North Vietnamese military operations against South Vietnam. As I have mentioned, estimates of the total tonnage required start at 15 tons per day of nonfood supplies. This can be quintupled and still be dwarfed by North Vietnam's actual imports of about 5,800 tons per day. And its import capacity is much greater. The ports together with the roads and railroads from China have an estimated capacity of about 14,000 tons a day.[31]

29. McNamara, *op. cit.*, p. 279.
30. *Ibid.*, p. 280.
31. *Ibid.*, p. 281.

Secretary McNamara ended up arguing that present bombing policy was appropriate for the goals the United States was pursuing and no other policy would do more. In the questioning Secretary McNamara denied the soundness of military propositions. Accelerated bombing in the past would not have resulted in fewer American casualties in the South. He denied that the costs of infiltration could have been made any higher.

> ...I don't believe there is any evidence that indicates that having accepted the Chiefs' recommendations at the time they were made as contrasted to acting on them later would have reduced the flow of men and materiel moving into South Vietnam from the North through Laos.[32]

He went on to argue that escalation in the North had reached its limits (civilian DM13) because of the risks of confrontation with the Soviet Union. Attacking another 57 targets, including the major ports, would be highly risky.[33] The JCS had argued that killing the same 57 targets would place political pressures on the adversary, although the Secretary interpreted their position as not implying that the war would necessarily be shortened.

McNamara said that he did not know if reducing the bombing would increase casualties in the South, because the air campaign did not really limit the flow of men and material into South Vietnam. It was rather the ability of the Viet Cong to integrate and deploy the flow of men and materiel. However, the secretary implied that he was not now in favor of a unilateral reduction without obtaining something substantial in return.

> I do know that in a sense to reduce the air campaign in the North gives the North Vietnamese a free ride on their aggression in the

---

32. *Ibid.*, p. 29.
33. *Ibid.*, p. 314.

South, and I would oppose it therefore unless we got something substantial in return for it.[34]

Senator Cannon cited the testimony of Generals Wheeler and McConnell that reduction of the bombing campaign would create fewer casualties in the South, and so Secretary McNamara was forced into direct disagreement.

Secretary McNamara: Yes, I read that testimony but I do not know what evidence they had to support that opinion.

Senator Cannon: But in any event you do not agree with them.
Secretary McNamara: I do not agree. I do not.[35]

Carrying out the strategy he felt was appropriate still left the length of the war undetermined. He could not predict when it would end.

The bombing went on in the fall of 1967 with additional pressure for removal of target prohibitions. Then target prohibitions were removed. Given that the actions implied by the military model had never been tried, and that the decisionmakers themselves predicted a long war, there would be military pressure for escalation even with increased risk of confrontation. At the same time, the constant military demand for more resources and growing public pressure against the war triggered a crisis over values as well as instruments.

The question of a change in bombing strategy without any Northern concession exercised the administration to the time President Johnson announced the bombing halt on March 31, 1968. Secretary McNamara in his final posture statement in February 1968 before Congress observed:

The systematic air campaign against fixed economic and military targets leaves few strategically important targets unstruck. Other

---

34. *Ibid.*, p. 316.
35. *Ibid.*, p. 319.

than manpower North Vietnam provides few direct resources to the war effort, which is sustained primarily by the large imports from the communist countries. The agrarian nature of the economy precludes an economic collapse as a result of the bombing. Moreover, while we can make it more costly in time and manpower, it is difficult to conceive of any interdiction campaign that would pinch off the flow of military supplies to the South as long as combat requirements remain as anything like the current low levels.[36]

If this were true, then, as noted in Chapter 3, there was little point to the bombing other than as a punitive device. The push for a bombing halt by some policymakers was foreshadowed in Clark Clifford's confirmation hearing just before Tet:

Senator Thurmond: When you spoke of negotiating, in which case you would be willing to have a cessation of bombing, I presume you would contemplate that they stop their military activities, too, in return for a cessation of bombing.

Mr.Clifford: No, that is not what I said. I do not expect them to stop their military activities....

Senator Thurmond: What do you mean by taking advantage of the pause in the bombing?

Mr. Clifford: Their military activity will continue in South Vietnam, I assume, until there is a cease fire agreed upon. I assume they will continue to transport the normal amount of goods, munitions, and men to South Vietnam. I assume that we will continue to maintain and support our forces during that period.[37]

---

36. McNamara (1969), p. 187.
37. Nomination of Clark M. Clifford to be Secretary of Defense. (1968, January 25). *Hearings Before the Committee on Armed Services, United States Senate.* Washington, DC: USGPO.

In other words, a bombing halt might be possible if the adversary implied that he would maintain the current "equilibrium" level of activity in the South.

After Tet and after General Westmoreland's troop requests came in, Secretary Clifford, as noted, began an overall review of Vietnam strategy that had the government in turmoil for a month. Meanwhile the president's outside senior advisory group weighed in with its recommendations for a partial bombing halt and stabilization of the ground war. (See Chapter 3.)

SUMMARY

This chapter has described a crisis over the volume of resources to be devoted to the war, not a crisis over how to achieve objectives for given levels of resources. The latter were delegated almost entirely to the military throughout the war. The controversies over resource levels occurred, because the propositions about military instruments in the decisionmakers' model and those in the military model were not truly competitive. Both parties had evolved a standard routine for handling requests for increased force levels. The civilian decisionmakers continually scaled down the requests from the "optimum" claimed by the military according to the standard incremental behavior in their proposition DM14 in explicit rejection of MM12 (that any requirements defined as necessary by the military should be met). This kind of routine still left everyone's propositions about strategy intact. Strategic propositions, concerning the effective use of military instruments, were never confronted with a systematic empirical test under agreed rules and evidence.[38] The quality of that evidence became

---

38. See Enthoven and Smith, *op. cit.*, p. 307.

more cloudy because of time and the disincentives for truth telling that now permeated the entire U.S. effort in Vietnam.

CHAPTER 5

MODERATE AND RADICAL DOVES

The first part of this chapter reviews the *Moderate Dove* model. Moderate Doves are the influential civilians who accepted the basic perceptions and views of the decisionmakers, but who came to believe the cost of the war was too high.[1] The second part reviews the *Radical Doves*, private actors who strongly opposed intervention in Vietnam from the start and who did so because they held "radical" views of the political and economic deficiencies of American society. By extension, any nation that was so deficient internally could never ever act correctly in the international arena.

Moderate Doves, like the decisionmakers makers from whom they evolved, analyzed the war with a priori models derived largely from their experience, using them to interpret the events of the war. They changed their models to fit the events only reluctantly and under the cumulative pressures of the events. In fact, Moderate Doves did not have to change their basic model very much, for it

---

1. Two species of Moderate Doves coexisted. *Old Doves* dissented from the very beginning of deep involvement in 1961. *New Doves* usually began their public dissent after they left government. Their opposition did not firm until 1966 or later. However, by 1968, the two species occupied the same intellectual terrain with respect to ending the war.

worked remarkably well in predicting the sequence of political and military outcomes in Vietnam. Compared with the accuracy of predictions, however, the action recommendations derived from the model did not work well whenever they were tried. For example, Dove models hold that negotiations with adversaries are always possible, because some common ground will always be revealed in going through the process. All principles and objectives are negotiable and malleable, if only there are adequate means of communication and each side understands the principles and objectives that drive the other side. Always failing negotiations could not refute the belief that negotiations are the only moral way to settle international differences. For Moderate and Radical Doves alike, morality and moral conduct are as much expected of nation-states as they are of individuals. For example, the strenuous efforts between 1968-1973 by the United States and third parties to end the war could only mean that the United States was not trying hard enough or was using the wrong model of national interest. In contrast, the grand marginalists Kissinger and Nixon viewed negotiations as more tit-for-tat, consistent with the pursuit of national interests within the tradition of great power politics.

The agreement between Moderate Dove predictions and actual outcomes in Vietnam did not result from sound practical knowledge about the causes and cures of insurgency. The value propositions in the Dove model have a pessimistic orientation toward the viability of any U.S. intervention abroad—particularly in the Third World. Dove models teach a universal lesson. Something will always go wrong in interventions. Foreign interventions anywhere are flawed. So models used to justify such interventions are inherently flawed. Events in Vietnam justified this pessimism.

The Doves argued that a much more accurate representation of the foreign policy process is contained in the following model. Many of its propositions are straight denials of those in the decisionmakers' basic model described in Chapter 3.

THE DOVE MODEL[2]

Although this model is more general and less articulated than that of the civilian decisionmakers, we can use a similar structure to classify the propositions in the Moderate Dove model.

A. United States Values and Interests

DoveM1. Definition: *American foreign policy should be oriented to "free nations," rather than to the smaller set in the "free world."*

Civilian decisionmakers and the military both defined the "free world" as that set of nations whose foreign policy was complementary to U.S. foreign policy. The free world, alternatively, was that set of nations whose foreign policy remained highly disjunct from the foreign policy of Soviet Union and China. In contrast, Doves defined the set of "free nations" by measuring their state of internal democracy and their rate of economic development. For them, India was the ideal free nation. It was nonaligned and so outside the distasteful cold war. It at least professed the ideals of social and economic democracy. It was internally democratic and used a recognizable voting system.

DoveM2. *Disengagement from the cold war is the prime U.S. foreign policy interest. While difficult, particularly in Western Europe, it was possible when dealing with free nations.*

DoveM3. *When national interests clash, such clashes will be partial at most and will be dominated by common interests, particularly the interest in peace.*

---

2. DoveM will denote the propositions in the Moderate Dove model.

DoveM3.1. *Negotiations with adversaries are always possible. Such negotiations resolve conflict by revealing and asserting dominance of common interests over parochial national interests.*

DoveM3.2. *The United Nations is a particularly important instrument for identifying common interests, and disputes between nations should be resolved there.*

DoveM4. Anti-domino theory: *Communism, democracy, or any other political forms are not automatically contagious from country to country.*

DoveM5. *The morale, confidence, and behavior of other nations in resisting communism have no relation to U.S. efforts to resist communism.*

DoveM5.1. Corollary: *There is no particular U.S. interest in confrontation per se. Tests of will by the U.S. against her adversaries are irrelevant to stability in free nations.*

DoveM6. *If the United States forecasts that an ally is unable to contain or defeat some communist insurgency, then there still is no requirement that the United States defeat it, particularly if the allied government is corrupt or despotic.*

B. The Irrelevance and Dangers of Military Force

DoveM7. *Military force is essentially irrelevant to the maintenance of U.S. interests in "free nations." This is particularly true in Asia.*

DoveM7.1. *Fighting a war on the Asian mainland is not feasible for the United States.*

DoveM7.2. *Military force used to induce compliance by an adversary is likely to have unintended or negative consequences.*

The liberal or rational attitude toward military policy must find its deepest foundation in an appreciation not simply of the costs and cruelties of war but of the essential irrelevance of the military problem to most of the real issues of the world we inhabit.[3]

...the most pressing issue is the Russian and Chinese challenge for the leadership of Asia and of Africa. If we are to meet it with reasonable success, we must, I am sure, abandon the notion that the Russian and Chinese revolutions can be reversed or that the spread of communism in the surrounding countries can be contained by giving armaments to the local military commanders and by establishing our own bases.[4]

DoveM8. *If conflict does occur there is a high probability that it will escalate to a very high, possibly nuclear level.*
DoveM8.1. *Combat in Asia creates a high probability of war with China and increases the probability of war with the Soviet Union.*

C. How Insurgency Conflicts Work Politically

DoveM9. Ways to win hearts and minds: *American resources should be allocated to capturing the "hearts and minds" of the people.* United States economic aid and Western democratic forms will cure the basic causes of insurgency: deep poverty and government repression.
DoveM9.1. Corollary: *The United States should never provide aid and comfort to indigenous corruption or despotism.*
DoveM10. A *positive relation exists between U.S. military and economic assistance used effectively in winning popular support and an allied government's morale and competence.* Popular support was a necessary condition for a competent government.
DoveM11. *Neither political effort nor economic effort by an ally is sufficient to defeat an insurgency. Both are necessary in an*

---

3. Millis (1962), p. 114.
4. Lippmann (1959), p. 41.

unspecified mix. Military instruments are marginally relevant at best.

D. How Policy Is Made

DoveM12. *Policy is made and changed incrementally.* Expecting either major reversals or major leaps forward is unrealistic. Tomorrow's policy will look much like today's. Changes are small ones in current directions.

E. Domestic Effects of War

DoveM13. *Military conflict abroad is corrupting internally for three reasons: (1) A large military establishment creates a domestic military mentality; (2) war abroad creates polarized attitudes at home; (3) military expenditures are diverted from domestic needs.*

CREATING A MODEL, 1961

Doves, like decisionmakers, did not worry much about Vietnam in 1961. For example, in the *Liberal Papers*, a 354-page Dove source book, Vietnam was the partial subject of a three-sentence section on Korea and Vietnam in an overall 48 page article by James Warburg (titled "A Reexamination of American Foreign Policy") and of an 18-page essay by Vera Michels Dean ("Southeast Asia and Japan").[5] The central point made by Doves who referred to Vietnam in more general discussions of broad U.S. policy was that the crucial matter was to capture the hearts and minds of the people (DoveM9).

> ...United States policy in Southeast Asia and Japan should have as its principal objective not the military build-up of the coun-

---

5. Roosevelt (1962).

admit of a conclusive "victory" in anything less than a decade—some experts say even longer.[9]

Six months later, another editorial in the same journal laid out with equal precision the future history of what would happen when a major escalation began, thus predicting events from 1965 through 1968. The article referred to:

> ...The French in 1946 estimated that it would take one-half million French troops to pacify Indochina. What it would take to "pacify" even South Vietnam today—after seven years of consolidation of Communist Viet Minh power in the north and with Chinese and Russian arsenals available—can hardly be projected in a tidy statistical estimate...
>
> If U. S. troops were made available to counter such a three-pronged offensive, certain consequences within the U. S. itself should be pondered. No tidy solution, a clear-cut "victory" is possible in this kind of fighting. And ever since Korea, the American people have been profoundly troubled by "victories" which turn out to be partial. A prolonged jungle war and loss of American lives would probably breed further frustration of the sort that gave rise to Joe McCarthy. This kind of popular reaction to an indecisive struggle could lead in either of two directions: to a new isolationism because "we are getting nowhere"; or, a panicky demand to "get it over with" which, in its crudest form, means dropping the H-bomb on Hanoi or Peking.[10]

The last paragraph is an explicit application of DoveM13, the negative domestic effects of foreign wars. Given such predictions, the most direct policy recommendation would be that intervention was infeasible. However, incrementalism (DoveM12) overcame

---

9. Commitment in Saigon. *(*1961, May 22*)*. *The New Republic*, pp. 3-4.

10. Going But Not Gone. (1961, November 6). *The New Republic*, pp. 4-5.

Dove fears. The Doves fell back on their belief in winning hearts and minds as a near cure-all (DoveM9). Winning hearts and minds required removing President Diem and his family and attacking pervasive GVN corruption.

> Though the present atmosphere of demoralization may lift momentarily in the wake of the [Vice President] Johnson visit, the stabilization of a non-Communist South Viet Nam depends, in the long run, on a rebirth of popular confidence in the Saigon regime. This quite obviously demands first, certain symbolic gestures indicative of a new departure: the removal of one Diem brother as grand vizier and of another as warlord of central Viet Nam, and of his sister-in-law as the palace agent in the National Assembly. Beyond this, however, the Diem regime should in our view reach out broadly to involve disaffected educated and middle class groups—especially leaders of those groups who are native to South as against North Viet Nam—and should even embrace some of the anti-Diem nationalists now in prison.[11]

A pseudonymous writer in *The New Republic*, but clearly one who had substantial and detailed acquaintance with Vietnam, summed up the need to move to a "hearts and mind" strategy:

> In South Vietnam, on the other hand, the United States seeks to win the struggle by mechanical means (helicopters and weed killers) forgetting all over again that a revolutionary war can be won only if the little people in the villages and the hills can be persuaded that they have a stake in fighting on our side. In South Vietnam, rather than "change horses" or even attempt to change the horse's manners, the United States has chosen to let it be led into midstream by the horse itself. In horsemanship, this is a

---

11. Commitment in Saigon. (1961, May 22). *The New Republic*, p. 5.

dangerous piece of foolishness. In the explosive situation in Vietnam, it can lead directly to another Korea.[12]

Such a "hearts and minds" prescription, however, was given a partial test. In November 1963, the horses were changed. With American acquiescence or connivance, Diem and his family were overthrown, and he and his brother were assassinated. What difference this made in actual popular support for the GVN is unrecorded. Since fighting continued, presumably, the little people in the society were not yet persuaded that they had a stake in "fighting on our side." Still more effort would be required to win hearts and minds just as the policy makers and the miliary believed that still more effort would be needed to attrit the Viet Cong and the NVA forces. This is the Dove form of sunk costs and necessary escalation—an open-ended commitment to winning hearts and minds. One final application of the Dove model in the new situation was the call for negotiations (Dove M3.1 and Dove M3.2).

> The immediate objective of a settlement might be a new strength-ened international presence—possibly under UN auspices—to seal the borders not only between North and South Vietnam but also North Vietnam and Laos. As presently constituted, the International Control Commissions now entrusted with this task under the 1954 Geneva Agreement are virtually powerless and might have to be superseded by a broadened international commission operating under new terms of reference.
>
> Though China cannot be trusted to respect for long a Swedish or Swiss-type neutrality of the states along her periph-ery, the chances for an "Austrian" solution fostered by a general international consensus are still open. It is the forming of such a consensus with the Russians, the Indians, the British, the French,

---

12. The War in Vietnam: We Have Not Been Told the Whole Story. (1962, March 20). *The New Republic*, p. 26.

and others that should in our view become the goal of United States policy.[13]

Any lack of interest in negotiation by the other side was not an admissible possibility. Subsequent history threw substantial doubt upon the potential attributed to such negotiations, although, as noted, an untested proposition can always be justified on an unresolvable "if only" basis. The failure of negotiations to achieve anything when they finally did get going from 1968 through 1973 cannot refute the proposition: if only the United States had tried negotiating in 1961.

1965

The 1964-1965 period was dominated by a sequence of moves by the adversary and U.S. countermoves. The Tonkin Gulf incident and the American bombing response; the mortaring of Pleiku; the much bigger bombing reaction to it, and, finally, the large increments in U.S. troop levels. The actual causal chain of the decisions over escalation was, of course, different from that implied by the temporal sequence of events. Rather than being a reaction to enemy attack, the escalation was primarily an attempt to bolster the GVN and deter the North from further involvement. Moderate Doves could only respond to the temporal sequence as publicly proclaimed by the Administration. The reaction had to be to the public sequence of events, not to the unknown or imperfectly known cause-effect chain actually operating.

The Doves' reactions to the escalation were slow at first, because the Tonkin Gulf incident took place during the Johnson-Goldwater presidential campaign. No Dove, of course, would see substitution of Goldwater for Johnson as a solution for administration errors. Consequently, the Moderate Doves gave the president the benefit of the doubt. If Johnson escalated this much, they

---

13. No Win in Vietnam. (1962, April 9). *The New Republic*, p. 5.

reasoned, imagine what Goldwater would have done. As put by the *New Republic*:

> The real lessons of Mr. Johnson's bit of brinkmanship are quite different from what the Goldwaterites suppose, and it is shuddersome to think what the results might have been had President Goldwater been in charge. Nothing was changed in the civil war in South Vietnam, where nothing can be achieved without the backing of the peasants, which is clearly not being got, or perhaps even sought. If the conditions of the war do change, it may be for the worse, since Chinese air power has been drawn into North Vietnam. All that the action in Tonkin Bay proves is that in a violent world there is a constant temptation to resort to force under provocation, but that the consequences are never predictable and the example is apt to be almost instantaneously contagious.[14]

After Johnson's landslide victory, however, the Doves, badly shaken by the escalation, could be far less restrained. The emphasis in the moderate Dove model shifted from the propositions toward the end of the list, concerning how to operate in a threatened allied nation to those at the beginning concerning United States world interests. For example, they invoked Proposition DoveM7, military forces are largely irrelevant; Proposition DoveM9, it is necessary to capture the hearts and minds of the people; Proposition DoveM10, United States resources can help gain popular support; Proposition DoveM11, political and economic methods are both needed

Winning hearts and minds still carried some force. The Diem regime had been followed by a series of generals, the current one at the time of escalation being Nguyen Khan. However, the Doves perceptions of corruption and disaffection increased. In fact, they saw the potential for corruption as ever increasing given the

---

14. Unmeasured Response. (1964, August 22). *The New Republic*, pp. 3-4.

increasing flow of American resources and the GVN's access to these resources. Disaffection with the GVN was encouraged, not only by corruption but also by the shifts in popular support toward the Viet Cong.

> Thanks to our military build-up we may no longer be losing the war in Vietnam as the French lost it; but the Viet Cong still exercise effective political control over a third to a half of the population of the South, manage to levy taxes of sorts in 41 of the South's 44 provinces, and do so with a military strength that the U.S. officially estimates at 140,000 or 165,000 men who are pitted against 600,000 South Vietnamese soldiers and 150,000 American ones...
>
> Oppressed subjects of despotic or corrupt Asian governments may seek relief from their woes by turning to some kind of Marxist-led movement.... But our armed forces cannot save governments from their own people, or prohibit others from making "unwise" political choices.[15]

The "hearts and minds"propositions were not denied, but they seemed less relevant as the United States engaged in open-ended escalation (DoveM8). Some writers took the trouble to make the Doves' propositions explicit, denying key assumptions of the decisionmakers' model, particularly Proposition DM4; denying the domino theory; and Proposition DM3, denying the U.S. interest in confrontation. According to Hans Morgenthau:

> ... the critical observer is struck by the motivating force which considerations of prestige exert both in Washington and Moscow. That this is so in Washington hardly needs extensive elaboration. 1f one probes beneath the rationalizations for our military presence in South Vietnam, one finds as the dominant motivation the fear that if South Vietnam should go Communist, no nation threatened by Communism would entrust its protection

---

15. Dare We Negotiate? (1965, November 6). *The New Republic*, p. 6.

to us. Thus one nation after the other would go Communist. In other words, the Communization of South Vietnam would be the beginning of the end of the free world. We have even dignified this historic determinism with the name of a theory, the so-called "Domino Theory." It assumes that as South Vietnam goes so will Thailand, and as Thailand goes so will India, and so forth, until the whole world will have gone Communist. This theory is a slogan born of fear and of a misconception of history and politics. It is unsupported by any historic evidence... [16]

But mainly it was the fear of escalation (DoveM8) at a time when they perceived the United States deliberately escalating, together with the open-endedness of the whole United States commitment to irrelevant military instruments (DoveM7) that were central to the reaction.

... There is talk of sending 100,000 or 300,000 Americans—and these figures assume that the enemy continues to be the 40,000 so-called hard core guerrillas and their 100,000 militarily active sympathizers, not the Russians, not the 400,000-strong North Vietnamese army, not the 2.5 million-strong Chinese army. Even granted this perhaps too optimistic assumption, that about the Administration's famed 10:1 ratio, regarded as essential for success against guerrillas? If the South Vietnamese military forces crack and the U. S. takes over more and more of the fighting, it will take, according to the ratio rule, about 1.5 million Americans five to 10 years to "win" a war that will stay "won" only so long as the American stay. [17]

Thus the Doves moved away incrementally during 1964-65 from the incrementalist position of "one step back" (DoveM12) and toward the more drastic recommendation of just getting out. The decisionmakers continued use of a model the Doves felt to be

---

16. Morgenthau (1965), p. 13.
17. The Sooner the Better. (1965, June 18). *The New Republic*, p. 6.

inappropriate led the latter toward the view that the preferred choice of instruments (that is, those to win hearts and minds) was no longer possible.The earlier Dove propositions on the U.S. interest in getting out of the cold war might require the abandonment of incrementalism in Vietnam, and, in fact, might require systemic change in U.S. foreign policy. The Doves, unlike the decisionmakers, went into crisis early. The crisis can be marked by looking at *The New Republic* editorials that bracketed the time. The earlier ones still talked of the importance of negotiations, although moving in the direction of withdrawal:

> The U.S. is committed to helping the Saigon government stay alive and has been doing so for 10 years. Neither President Johnson nor his predecessors, however, have been committed to doing for the Vietnamese what they will not or cannot do for themselves...
> ... the logical alternative is to suggest to South Vietnam that it seek peace...[18]

By the end of this time period, however, when the number of U. S. troops was mounting fast and American forces were in combat, getting out had become the principal Dove policy preference. Negotiations were still important, but they were negotiations clearly expected to preserve little, except some United States "face."

> We have not given up hope that this acceleration toward a major Asian war can be reversed in 1966—if the Administration is willing to give more serious consideration to Ho Chi Minh's proposals than it has so far done. Granted that many South Vietnamese Catholics and Buddhists are at least as opposed to a Communist regime as they so often have been to the successive regimes in Saigon, perhaps some refugee plan could be worked

---

18. Vietnam—What Now. (1966, January 8). *The New Republic*, p. 4.

Out for them, on the lines of what we offered Cubans wanting to get away from Castro. But a Communist-dominated Vietnam need not be merely a tool of China.[19]

The Doves continued to look for negotiated solutions until negotiations began in 1968. Dove ranks were augmented by a flow of officials out of the administration. Released from official responsibilities, they were moving from a war fighting to a negotiating strategy. Many opposed escalation and bombing. Beginning about fall 1965 Secretary McNamara, had become an emergent Dove.

1968

Events up to 1968 came close to what had been predicted by the Moderate Doves since 1961. Even high technology, elaborate U.S. military forces could not defeat the insurgency (DoveM7). Military escalation was inevitable (DoveM8). The United States could never capture the hearts and minds of the people (Proposition Dove M9).

Negotiations remained the most important objective in 1968 as it was in 1965. Negotiating well required physical presence, and so Doves did not advocate immediate unilateral withdrawal. Proposition Dove M9, the hearts and minds proposition with its corollary opposition to despotism, led them to favor a broad-based coalition, including the Viet Cong. Doves believed the Thieu-Ky government certainly met the criteria for despotism. Whether such a coalition was to be adopted to get negotiations going or was to be a result of negotiations was never clear nor agreed. It was as much as anything the basis of the small differences between the two Dove Senators running for president—Robert Kennedy and Eugene McCarthy.

---

19. Johnson's Choice. (1966, January 8). *The New Republic*, p. 10.

What mattered in 1968, was the internal state of the nation, which was approaching a crisis over the war. The undesirable domestic impact of interventions had always been implicit in Dove policy recommendations. Now there was a much stronger appeal to basic American values and the need for a new set of priorities.

During March 1968, a month of crisis for the decisionmakers reconsidering their model, Senator Fulbright said:

> The crisis over the war at home is the result of certain striking discrepancies—discrepancies between events and the description of them by the Administration, between current Administration policies and traditional American values.[20]

And in June, Senator McCarthy said:

> ... I think that in this year I sensed what the country needed. Namely, that it needed and wanted a challenge to the President of the United States on the policies of Vietnam and priority for America.[21]

THE EVOLUTION OF ADMINISTRATION HAWKS INTO MODERATE DOVES

The new Moderate Doves now felt free to advocate the singular importance of winning the hearts and minds of the people

> Much more devotion and intelligence are at present going into the programs of reconstruction and pacification. But two factors hold up the social revolution in South Vietnam: the capacity of the enemy to slice through so much of the country with relative immunity; and, equally important, the resistance of the large landholders and leading elements in the Saigon government to

---

20. Fulbright, W. J. (1968, March 12). *New York Times*.
21. McCarthy, E. (1968, June 3). Kennedy-McCarthy Debate. *New York Times*.

any serious programs of social reform. In any case, as claimants
on our resources, these programs are hopelessly outclassed by
the programs of destruction...[22]

These new Moderate Doves also opposed the bombing, but
they did so "responsibly." They were against further bombing of
the North. However, they remained committed to some military
force, because they believed that U.S. willingness to increase its
sunk costs mattered in maintaining the free world and winning the
cold war.

This "mixed" model embraced propositions from both the
decisionmakers and the Doves. Whenever the propositions of the
decisionmakers and the Moderate Doves did not conflict, former
decisionmakers and government officials would accept them.
Whenever they conflicted, the former Hawks inclined toward
Moderate Dove positions, but not to dismissing U.S. objectives or
the use of force to achieve them. Thus, from the decisionmakers'
model we have:

DM1. A gain for the Communists is a loss for the United
States.

DM2. The domino theory.

DM3. The relation between demonstrations of United States
resolve and allied morale and competence.

DM5. The need to defeat Communist insurgencies.

DM6. Communist insurgencies require outside help.

DM7. Adversaries receiving U.S. signals through U.S. inputs.

DM9. Defeating an insurgency requires military and political
efforts.

DM12. The U.S. ability to conduct military operations in an
insurgent environment.

---

22. Schlesinger (1967), p. 61.

However, acceptances of these DM propositions were now compatible with accepting the following proposition from the Old Doves' model.

DoveM2. On the need to get out of the cold war.

DoveM8. On the inherent escalation involved in military conflict.

DoveM9. The need to win hearts and minds and not to support corrupt despotic regimes.

DoveM10. On the positive relation between U.S. resources devoted to gaining popular support and allied morale and competence.

DoveM11. On the need for political and economic measures in an unspecified mix. As put by Schlesinger apparently with some inner tension:

> I think a middle course is still possible if there were the will to pursue it. And this course must begin with a decision to stop widening and Americanizing the war—to limit our forces, actions, goals and rhetoric. Instead of bombing more places, sending in more troops, proclaiming even more ardently that the fate of civilization will be settled in Vietnam, let us recover our cool and try to see the situation as it is: a horrid civil war in which communist guerrillas, enthusiastically aided and now substantially directed from Hanoi, are trying to establish a communist despotism in South Vietnam, not for the Chinese but for themselves. Let us understand that the ultimate problem here is not military but political. Let us adapt the means we employ to the end we seek.[23]

Or according to Goodwin:

> Our future policy in Vietnam must follow two parallel roads—the road of negotiation and the road of combat. Past

---

23. Schlesinger, *op. cit.*, pp.105-106.

miscalculation should have humbled us to the awareness that each specific step may have larger consequences than we can foresee. Each should be tested against a single standard: Does it serve or injure the bedrock vital interest of the United States? That interest is to establish that American military power, once committed to defend another nation, cannot be driven from the field. It is not to guarantee South Vietnam forever against the possibility of a Communist takeover.[24]

The most specific military/strategic interpretation of this was by General James M. Gavin, whose "enclave strategy" of continuing to hold small heavily defended areas on the Vietnamese coast, combined the refusal to withdraw derived from incrementalism (one step back) with the fear of escalation of Dove M8. The enclaves were an attempt to hold a military position in Vietnam, but to put an absolute limit on that position so that further escalatory commitments would cease.

...If our objective is to secure all of South Vietnam, then forces should be deployed on the 17th parallel and along the Cambodian border adequate to do this. In view of the nature of the terrain, it might be necessary to extend our defenses on the 17th parallel to the Mekong River, and across part of Thailand. Such a course would take many times as much force as we now have in Vietnam.

On the other hand, if we should maintain enclaves on the coast, desist in our bombing attacks in North Vietnam, and seek to find a solution through the United Nations or a conference in Geneva we could very likely do so with the forces now available.[25]

---

24. Goodwin (1966), p. 38.
25. Gavin (1966, February), pp. 16-17.

RADICAL DOVES

The Radical Dove model differs significantly from all other
Vietnam models. The basic propositions are not "marginal" ones
as in the other models. Models that are marginalist in spirit try to
find improvements on substance and process that are not far away
from the current status quo. However, radical models hold that
there are flaws in the deep structure of the status quo that
marginalists refuse to consider. Radical models present a moral
critique of American society and derive policy from that critique.
Nonmarginal models were unlikely to affect the kinds of policies
typically pursued by the Vietnam decisionmakers. Political and
bureaucratic systems that operate slowly, according to well defined
standard operating procedures, find it difficult to cope with drastic
alternatives.

Understanding the Radical Dove model and its application to
the Vietnam conflict is important for two reasons. First, promoters
of the model were voluble enough so that they affected the political
context within which decisionmakers were making policy. At the
beginning of the Vietnam conflict, civilian decisionmakers
attached low weight to domestic consequences of limited war. The
radical discussion of the war aided in changing the weight the
decisionmakers had given to winning the war. The decisionmakers
believed, emotionally as well as rationally, in the domino theory
and that they would be held responsible if the dominoes fell on
their watch.

The Radical Dove alternative made the Moderate Dove model
seem incremental. The decisionmakers could accept limits on their
investment in Vietnam and see the need to negotiate a way out as
suggested by the Moderate Dove model. The Radical Dove model
differed from the others primarily on values. Values are ordinarily
taken as given in the realm of "rational" or analytical debate. The
radicals saw the decisionmakers as attempting to monopolize
"rational" or "responsible" discourse over the war. The unwilling-
ness of the decisionmakers to consider the values of the radicals
led the latter to a view of the American political system as

unresponsive—in some cases so unresponsive as to be immoral. They made no allowance for the fact that value-laden argument is a difficult tool with which to affect the conduct of public policy directly.

THE RADICAL DOVE MODEL

The following propositions make up the Radical Dove model:[26]

RDoveM1. *National interest does not exist, only the interest of humanity. Actions must be valued and judged on the basis of their effects on people. Who and where the people are is irrelevant.*

In the moderate Dove model moderates agreed with the decisionmakers that national interests were important but disagreed strongly both about what these interests were and how to maintain them. The Radical Doves models differed from the moderates as well as the decisionmakers on basic expressed values, although there was some agreement with the moderates on how things work.

RDoveM2. The radicals agreed with the moderate Doves on the irrelevance of the domino theory (DoveM4).

RDoveM3. Radical Doves agreed with Moderate Doves that there was no requirement for the United States to defeat communist insurgencies (DoveM6).

RDoveM4. Radical Doves and Moderate Doves agreed on the irrelevance of military force in combating indigenous insurgencies (DoveM7).

RDoveM5. Radical Doves and Moderate Doves agreed on the dangers of escalation whenever military force was used (DoveM 8).

---

26. We use RDoveM to denote the propositions in the Radical Dove model.

Radical Doves took issue, however with some of Moderate Dove operational propositions. Radical Doves believed that indigenous revolution was a legitimate policy tool to solve Third World problems, although they balked at revolutions induced by external agents.

RDoveM6. *Revolution may be the only way to solve the Third World problem, and perhaps elsewhere. If such revolution turns out to be communist-led, this is, at worst, much the least of a number of evils.*[27]
RDoveM6.1. *U.S. efforts to resist communism actually encouraged communism, because they meant U.S opposition to popular revolution.*

Moderate Doves held that the morale, confidence, and behavior of nations in resisting communism had no positive or negative relation to U. S. efforts.

RD6.2. *Men of good will and humanity should frequently encourage revolution in Third World nations.*

This differed from Moderate Dove Propositions 9 to 11, which summarize the "hearts and minds" doctrine for defeating insurgency.

RDoveM6.3. *Radical alternative policies are not only necessary but the only viable ones; anything less is mere surface change.*

This view differed, of course, from the incrementalism of Moderate Dove Proposition 12.

---

27. But note that many of the radicals were anti-communists of long standing.

RDoveM6.4. *Radical alternatives are necessary at home as well as abroad.*

This was markedly different from the Moderate Dove argument that military conflict abroad is bad, because it polarizes at home (DoveM13). The radicals wanted polarization; they formed one pole.

The Radical Doves held the following views on how policy is made:

RDoveM7. *Policymakers define and control the range of "thinkable" options for the United States. There is no necessary policy justification or moral justification for the range of options selected. They are determined by irrelevant historical, organizational, and class factors.*

RDoveM7.1. *Decisionmakers will always deceive the people in a democracy about the true reasons for their behavior.*

RDoveM7.2. Guide for radical conduct: *It is the obligation of radicals to pursue options beyond the "permissible" (by moderate definition) ranging up to the point where one's own means become immoral (according to humanistic traditions).*

The crucial difference between the Radical Dove model and all the others is that radical models contained a whole set of propositions not found in any other models. Radical Dove models contained internal value judgments about how things should work. Moderate Doves ran their external general value judgments through their assessments of the way the political and military world worked empirically, and they arrived at policy actions and recommendations. The Radical Doves did not like the way the world worked, and their model included propositions about how it should work. A humanistic moral calculus had to be applied directly to individual actions and to the actions of one's own nation. Bad actions were to be avoided, good ones advocated, and morally better ones carried out instead of morally poorer ones.

RDoveM8.1. *An absolute moral calculus should be applied, in
the first instance, to one's own personal actions, and, in the second
instance, to the actions of one's country.*

Corollary RDoveM8.1. *The existence of an opponent who is
taking actions even more immoral than one's own or those of one's
country is not relevant to the morality of one's own personal
actions or to the actions of the United States.*

An absolute morality meant putting the major stress on the
morality of immediate actions rather than ultimate outcomes. It led
to advocating nonviolence by most Radical Doves in most
circumstances, even by some of the ones that truly believed in the
necessity of revolution. By and large Radical Doves agreed with
Moderate Doves on their gloomy assessment of the ultimate
outcome of existing policies. However, even if they had disagreed,
to be consistent, they would have opposed existing policies
because of the immediate immorality of the actions the government
was taking.

THE REACTION TO ESCALATION: 1965-1966

Before 1961 there were no radical Dove views on Vietnam per
se. A radical Dove model evolved as a response to the war and to
the perceived behavior of the Kennedy and Johnson administrations. After the bombings began early in 1965 there was an attempt
to divine the "true" reasons for American behavior (RDoveM 7.1).

As long as the official Washington line was that the war was
going well, there was at least a suggested recognition that the
war was essentially a civil war, and the Viet Cong an indigenous
movement, aided and abetted by Hanoi. President Kennedy many
times implicitly accepted this view in statements the war must be
won in the South and by the South Vietnamese.

Once Washington abandoned the view that any United States-
organized Saigon regime could defeat the Viet Cong and vast

numbers of U.S. combat troops were committed to the war, a new reality had to be fabricated. The Johnson Administration now denied the reality of a civil war and advanced the notion that the war was the result of "aggression" by a foreign power— North Vietnam.[28]

> The question is why would the administration want to withhold the truth. What purpose would it serve. ...The only conceivable explanation is that there is a contradiction between the stated aims of the government and its real aims.[29]

The "true" reason for the decisionmakers' behavior was an irrational anti-Communism plus a United States propensity to imperialism. Both of these propensities could be judged as bad international politics and as immoral. Further, they increased the likelihood of communism (RDoveM6.1)

> And what majority exists for the Vietnam policy is glued together on the whole by an anti-Communism of a reactionary type. It is ready to support fascist dictatorships, overthrow democratic regimes, or go to the nuclear brink—all in the name of an anti-Communist crusade. It is paradoxically the kind of anti-Communism on which Communism thrives, since it contributes to the social and political climate where those in opposition or rebellion against existing social conditions can be misled to the conclusion that their only choice is between a reactionary status quo which they experience in their daily lives backed by the U. S in the name of anti-Communism or support of a Communist-movement which speaks in the name of freedom.[30]

---

28. Bottone (1965), p. 6.
29. Lens (1966), p. 17.
30. Bottone (1965), *op cit.*, p. 8.

Our whole policy in Vietnam makes us appear as the imperial
ists, and white imperialists at that.[31]

Propositions RDoveM8 and RDoveM8.1 on the morality of
means appear even more clearly in the following passage from the
Christian Century. What matters in this passage is the immorality
of intervening where there has been no request from the people.
The effect of such immorality destroys the intervener as well as
those who suffer the effects.

Anyone who suggests a clear moral judgment on Vietnam must
expect to be accused of "moralism"—a naive and dangerous
confusion of politics and morality. A moral judgment, however,
is very different from a moralistic one. The morality upon which
my condemnation of American policy is based involves a search
for principles which apply to everyone, including ourselves in a
specific situation.

We have no right to intervene in the affairs of other nations
to give them what *we* conceive as a good government. We do
have a responsibility as great as our enormous capacity for
mischief: to refrain from (and prevent American private interests,
from strengthening bad governments. We certainly have no right
to keep another people from getting rid of an oppressive government or of traditional patterns of exploitations.

Great evil has arisen from the fact that American policy in
Vietnam has been moralistic rather than moral. That policy has
been rationalized by the assertion that communists are acting in
Vietnam, that communists have evil intentions and must always
be stopped by the American government, that since our ends are
good they justify whatever means are necessary to realize them.
It has been rationalized by rhetorical appeals to moral principles
which we ourselves ignore and block. And peace has been
offered to those we have invaded on condition that they cease

31. Thomas (1965), p. 8.

resistance. If we continue to confuse morality and moralism, Vietnam will prove only the beginning of national disaster.[32]

The perception of the immoral effects of the war on U. S. international conduct and on the Vietnamese people were matched by perceptions of immoral consequences at home. The war was delaying the needed reconstruction of American domestic affairs (RDoveM 6.4)

> What are we doing to ourselves? Only now in the escalating viciousness of the Vietnam can the vigorous civil rights worker be crushed along the pacifists, students, scholars, and critics alike energy is best destroyed in a general foray. My great fear as the Vietnam engagement escalates is the political repression that will go on here at home.[33]

At the end of his "empirical" analysis and "predictions," Kotler searches for the moral stand that Radical Doves feel is necessary for complete political statements.

> What side do we take then? Those of us who don't want empire, but instead a hundred zoos in the city and children learning life science, getting dollars to be zookeepers. Those of us who want neighborhood community and a hundred theaters in our cities. And hostelries for students traveling across the country to do good work. Those of us who want community in the city and politics of self-governing decision and action. And a law upon which the art of wisdom can grow. Those of us who want a joyous church. Those of us who want to laugh and love, and feel kinship with our neighbor. Will Vietnam do this? Or will it make us more sterile and our public life and mind more impoverished?
> Do we say goodbye to republic and now welcome empire? What side do we take, without destroying our spirit, our love, our past, and the rejoicing vision with which this nation began? How

---

32. Harris (1965), pp. 1156-1157.
33. Kotler (1965), p. 14.

must we view McNamara's charts and the military money changers.[34]

In 1965 the moral stand was not yet fully articulated, but it implied that the United States should get out. The political and moral damage it was doing to itself and Vietnam was far greater than the damage that would result from Vietnam going communist (RDoveM6). Responsible action involved *not* trying to discuss alternatives within the government's framework, but maximizing protest against the framework (Proposition RDoveM7.2—the obligation to pursue options beyond those of the government).

> All of us who want an end to our war have a responsibility to maximize our protest, not to draft alternative policies. If we can make our protest significant, and that protest buttresses the growing outcry and outrage against our Vietnam war, the Administration (pressured by a deteriorating international situation) might decide to withdraw. Strategists and similar experts will then be charged to devise a policy for withdrawal which saves maximum "face." (Witness the process of our decision not to press for payment of the Soviet Union's debt to the U. N.). Saving "face" is the Administration's problem, as is the definition of the appropriate policy. I'd get out now and lose all "face"...[35]

> Why do we think that, even if we miraculously win a military victory over the Vietcong—which now after ten years of massive American economic—military support to its enemies, controls most of the country—our army of occupation can set up and sustain a viable non-Communist government, assuming there is much left to govern after our bombings? And finally, why are we asked whether we "really care what happens to the people of Southeast Asia so long as America gets out?" The question is not

34. *Ibid.*, p. 15.
35. Fruchter (1965, Fall), p. 624.

what will or may happen to those people, but what is happening to them so long as America stays in.[36]

There were better countries to defend. It was a practical policy which might in practice have worked or not worked, but the new policy, the policy of escalation, is a radical policy; it is a policy of the radical right, right out of the naked lunching heart of the Wasp in his fevers. For no one can know, not even Johnson himself, if escalation is our best defense against Communism, a burning of orphans to save future orphans, or if the war is the first open expression of a totalitarian Leviathan which will yet dominate everything still not nailed down in American life...[37]

THE LOGIC OF WITHDRAWAL: 1967-1968

In 1965, the various Radical Dove beliefs had not yet been ordered and put into a coherent argument for withdrawal. Two scholars, historian Howard Zinn and linguist Noam Chomsky accomplished this in 1967 and 1968. Their work sums up the whole Radical Dove position and attempts to clarify the logic of such models. This inquiry into alternative models of the Vietnam War, therefore, ends by considering their two major works on the subject: Zinn, *Vietnam: The Logic of Withdrawal* and Chomsky, *American Power and the New Mandarins*.[38]

Zinn and Chomsky both begin with the warrants for their competence to address the issues. First, the judgment and analysis of the war do not depend on facts available only to the decision-makers, but on the theory or model that puts the facts into context. The appropriate model to be used contains moral propositions.

... making moral judgments—as on the war in Vietnam—does not depend mainly on the volume of our knowledge. We find,

---

36. Macdonald (1965, Fall), p. 638.
37. Mailer (1965, Fall), p. 642.
38. Beacon Press, Boston, and Vintage Books, New York, 1969.

indeed, that the experts in each field disagree sharply on the most fundamental questions. This is because ethical decisions depend on the relationships in which we place the facts we know. Therefore, what we bring to the common body of evidence on Vietnam—the *perspective* we have—is crucial.[39]

In particular, if there is a body of theory, well tested and verified, that applies to the conduct of foreign affairs or the resolution of domestic or international conflict, its existence has been kept a well guarded secret. In the case of Vietnam, if those who feel themselves to be experts have access to principles or information that would justify what the American Government is doing in that unfortunate country, they have been singularly ineffective in making this known.[40]

Having established the competence of the Radical Doves to address Vietnam issues, Zinn moves onto analysis. In line with the anti-nationalistic orientation of the Radical Dove model, he notes that the United States is an imperialist nation, although no more than others, certainly no better.

I will offer a proposition which I believe modern history supports with a great deal of evidence: that no great power can be trusted—not Germany, Italy, Japan; not Russia, not France, not England, not the United States—when freedom and self-determination for other nations are at stake. ... We have been as gullible as citizens of other countries in believing the statements of leaders, and just as careless in neglecting to match these statements against the actual behavior of our nation.[41]

Zinn and Chomsky then go on to their version of the American propensities for anticommunist crusades (RDoveM6).

---

39. Zinn, p. 4.
40. Chomsky, pp. 342-343.
41. Zinn, *op. cit.*, p. 28.

Each succeeding argument comes closer and closer to what post-war history shows to be the core principle of United States foreign policy; that somehow—we must "stop communism." This belief is not questioned or examined; it has become a matter of faith. It does not come from a rational study of communism in its complexities and contradictions, it changes over time, it moves—from monolith to bipolarity, to multipolarity. It is not informed by the work on communism produced by the nation's scholars. We have here a reflex action conditioned over a long period of time, so that any warning of "communism," however faint or uncertain, brings a violent response.[42]

In its anticommunist crusade the United States inflicts damage on the population it purports to save, but the damage counts very little in the calculations of decisionmakers.

... when no one can tell the difference between a farmer and a Viet Cong and the verdict is guilty until proved innocent, then the mass killing of civilians is inevitable. It is not deliberate. But neither is it accidental. It is not part of the war and so discardable. It is the war.[43]

I suppose this is the first time in history that a nation has so openly and publicly exhibited its own war crimes. Perhaps this shows how well our free institutions function. Or does it simply show how immune we have become to suffering.?[44]

The damage inflicted on an indigenous population is the cost to them of the United States maintaining a regime the people do not want and can in no way be justified as representative. It is in fact evil.

How can American support for such governments be justified? To some it hardly needs justification; anything is

---

42. Zinn, *op. cit.*, p. 84.
43. Zinn, *op. cit.* p. 61
44. Chomsky, *op. cit*, p. 10.

preferable to communism—even a dictatorship based on a wealthy elite controlling impoverished masses. American liberals, however, cannot accept this at first. They must seek a third way so that our foreign policy can satisfy the aims of liberty and justice and the rest. What they refuse to grasp is that where a third way is indeed feasible, it cannot be manufactured and exported like Coca-Cola.... Refusing to accept these limits to what an outsider can do, the United States engages in a giant pretense. It announces that reform is on the way, then it entrusts the carrying out of that reform to those very people who constitute the right-wing elites of wealth—those who have most to lose by change.[45]

Nor is it obscure why the American government continues to use its military force to impose on the people of Vietnam the regime of the most corrupt, most reactionary elements in Vietnamese society. There is simply no one else who will do its bidding and resist the overwhelming popular sentiment for peace, and no doubt neutralism.[46]

However, the damage that the United States inflicts on itself is as great as that it inflicts on Vietnam.

The Negro compares the magnitude of national effort to bring what is claimed to be "freedom" to 13 million people in South Vietnam with the magnitude of the effort for 15 million Negroes who are poor at home. He compares the $2 billion spent each month on the war with the pitiful sums of money spent on behalf of the Negro...[47]

The health of our system would have been demonstrated by a change of policy caused by a recognition that what we have done in Vietnam is wrong, a criminal act, that an American "victory" would have been a tragedy. Nothing could be more remote from

45. Zinn, *op. cit*, p. 45.
46. Chomsky, *op. cit.*, p. 230
47. Zinn, *op. cit.*, p. 23.

the American political consciousness. So long as this remains true, we are fated to relive this horror.[48]

Because of the physical and moral costs to everyone involved, Zinn and Chomsky both come to feel that unilateral American withdrawal was the only reasonable course.

History does not show that a nation which liquidates a bad venture suffers a serious loss of prestige where it can compensate in other ways. Proud, powerful England surrendered to the ragtag thirteen American colonies, removed her armed forces ignominiously, and did not suffer for it. More recently, and more pertinently, France moved out voluntarily from Algeria and from Indochina. Today she has more prestige than ever before. The Soviet Union pulled her missiles out of Cuba; her prestige has not suffered. There is a kind of prestige this nation should not worry about losing—that which is attached to sheer power, to victory by force of arms, devoid of moral content. Which is more terrible: to have people in the world say that the United States withdrew from an untenable situation, or to have it said, as is now being said everywhere, that the United States is acting foolishly and immorally in Vietnam?[49]

What would be the consequences of a withdrawal of American forces from Vietnam? If past events are any guide, the cessation of aggressive military action by the United States will lead to a disengagement of North Vietnamese units, as happened, apparently, during the bombing pause in January 1966. It is noteworthy that no group in South Vietnam has advocated North Vietnamese involvement in an immediate political solution, and the same North Vietnamese leadership that was willing, a decade ago, to arrange a modus vivendi with Diem would very likely agree to negotiate the problems of Vietnam with a government

---

48. Chomsky, *op. cit.*, p. 11.

49. Zinn, p. 108. Note that Zinn's ability to predict the actual behavior of the North Vietnamese when the American "occupation" ended was very limited in the short- and the long-run.

that would at least respond to its diplomatic notes. Just what might emerge from the shattered debris of South Vietnamese society, no one can predict with any confidence. It is clear, however, that under the American occupation there can be only unending tragedy.[50]

In a comment written after the Tet offensive, Chomsky makes a final recommendation for those in the peace movement that sums up his views and those of the Radical Doves criticizing American liberals—our Moderate Doves—on their role in the war and for their dishonesty in refusing to recommend unilateral withdrawal on grounds of national interest. It seems fitting to use this recommendation as the summary of this chapter.

Nevertheless, those who have devoted themselves to working for peace in Vietnam can only be saddened by the realization that they have failed to create the consciousness in this country that we have no right to win a military victory. It is the miraculous heroism of the Vietnamese resistance that has forced these tentative moves towards peace in Vietnam. To say this is not to make a political judgment with regard to the various forces in Vietnamese society, but only to recognize the bare and inescapable facts. For the so-called "peace movement," the recent events pose a major challenge. The "peace movement" has been getting by for too long with cheap jokes about LBJ and with concentration on peripheral issues such as the bombing of North Vietnam. The challenge it now faces is to create the understanding that we have no right to set any conditions at all on a political settlement in Vietnam; that American military force must be withdrawn from Vietnam, and from the other simmering Vietnams throughout the world; that American power and resources and technical skills must be used to build and not to repress or to "contain" or to destroy.[51]

---

50. Zinn, p. 108.
51. Chomsky, *op. cit.*, p. 275.

CHAPTER 6

THE TRAGEDY OF POLICY MODELS

Assume that the United States' minimal objectives, (1) deterring the Soviet Union and China from undertaking interventions in the Third World, and (2) preventing the overthrow of democratic governments by force were sound as defined by traditional norms for American decisionmakers. Then the primary failure of their model lay not in its objectives, but in its factual propositions about how conflict works in the Third World. The decisionmakers inferred the wrong lessons of history. Their model emphasized conventional military force too much. Maladroit strategy and tactics and a maladapted force structure combined to produce a cost-ineffective prosecution of a "necessary" war. The United States applied military force in the wrong way, because the decisionmakers and the generals were all captives of times and circumstances when that same type of force had proved itself a winner. They used the history of previous conflicts in such a crude way that they could not distinguish between the factors that had led to winning in the past and their potential absence in the immediate conflict.

The military naturally used the force structure that the decisionmakers had provided. The generals applied their own lessons from history and their own well-developed theory of conflict. Their theory of conflict and on the winning uses of violence stood at variance with the sophisticated signaling theory the decisionmakers believed they were applying.

The two Dove models tell us that failure in Vietnam was inevitable, because all such interventions are immoral. Immorality makes interventions infeasible. The United States should never have intervened in 1961, or having erroneously intervened, should have gotten out in 1965 rather than escalating. From the Dove perspective, the decisionmakers' model failed, because it contained improper values. Ineffective pursuit of immoral policies was evil, but effective pursuit would have been more evil. Because all parties to the conflict could perceive this evil, it followed that intervention would be ineffective.

Such conflicting models raise a central question. How can these a priori policy models, gross and coarse suspensions of values, unverifiable facts, and untestable forecasts be brought into question earlier? Political and military shocks and obvious failure may provide catalysts for policy revision, but not always.[1] Sometimes they generate more effort to win because of individual decision biases and group pathologies. The decisionmakers' model was questioned early and often, from the outside, but the outside questioning was never taken seriously.

Although the decisionmakers despised the alternative values proposed by the Radical Doves, they came closest to the fundamental criticism necessary to confront ingrained policy models. However, criticism derived from basic propositions about collective or personal morality is not likely to be given much weight in any public decisionmaker's calculus. Certainly, decisionmakers are

---

1. Public sector policy analysts and private sector management scientists both believe that by analyzing actual organizational failures and pathologies they can draw lessons about avoiding them in the future. See, for example, Hogwood and Peters (1985). Conversely, they believe that they can find generalizable examples of organizational success that can identify learning, good practice and benchmarks for organizations that desire to be successful in the future. See, for example, Cohen and Sproull (1996).

not likely to get fundamental questioning from their subordinate bureaus. Policy models become "endogenized." Inside U.S. government bureaus, people who produce moral arguments for or against pending policy alternatives will only damage their own careers and reduce the present and future resources their bureaucracies can expect.

The decisionmakers' model incorporated the lessons democracies believed they had learned about the need to resist threats of aggression early and to fight actual aggression with maximum available resources. Their model rested on an assumed, but forever unprovable, counterfactual that World War II would not have occurred without Neville Chamberlain's appeasement of Hitler at Munich or would have been won in far easier fashion with some other policy. By analogy, "appeasement" in Vietnam or even a basic strategy of negotiation with the North Vietnamese would never bring lasting peace. President Johnson set the tone at the top by combining the Munich analogy with a literal domino theory. For example:

> We did not choose to be the guardians at the gate, but there is no one else. Nor would surrender in Viet-Nam bring peace, because we learned from Hitler at Munich that success only feeds the appetite of aggression. The battle would be renewed in one country and then another country, bringing with it perhaps even larger and crueler conflict, as we have learned from the lessons of history.[2]

By forcing his rhetoric into the government's strategic planning process, the President made his model the government's model. For example, National Security Action Memorandum 288, in a tone of desperation, delivers the entire model very compactly in the following passage:

---

2. Johnson, L. B., Pres. (1965, July 28). Statement. White House news conference.

Unless we can achieve this objective in South Vietnam, almost all of Southeast Asia will probably fall under Communist dominance (all of Vietnam, Laos, and Cambodia), accommodate to Communism so as to remove effective United States and anti-Communist influence (Burma), or fall under the domination of forces not now explicitly Communist but likely then to become so (Indonesia taking over Malaysia). Thailand might hold for a period without help, but would be under grave pressure. Even the Philippines would become shaky, and the threat to India on the West, Australia and New Zealand to the South, and Taiwan, Korea, and Japan to the North and East would be greatly increased.

All of these consequences would probably have been true even if the United States had not since 1954, and especially since 1961, become so heavily engaged in South Vietnam. However, that fact accentuates the impact of a Communist South Vietnam not only in Asia but in the rest of the world, where the South Vietnam conflict is regarded as a test case of United States capacity to help a nation to meet the Communist "war of liberation."

Thus, purely in terms of foreign policy, the stakes are high....[3]

As they agonized over their self-created and self-bounded choices and tried to set an effective policy on Vietnam, none of the major decisionmakers stopped to probe the basic assumptions of their model, its action implications, or its potential costs. For example, a strict "lessons of Munich" model contains no conditional statements about any need for domestic political support. Costs are not important in resisting aggression of Hitlerian magnitude, and so there is no need to produce estimates about the costs appropriate to resist "ordinary" aggression. No one conducted any sensitivity analysis to see how robust some Munich-derived model could be if there were huge departures from its basic

---

3. NSAM 288 (1964, March 17). Document #64: United States Objectives in Vietnam. In Sheehan et al. (1971), p. 284.

premises. The decisionmakers did not ask about the flexibility they would retain if the evolving military and political facts on the ground suggested they were using the wrong analogies and drawing the wrong historical lessons. They remained always remarkably ignorant of the constraints local history might place on the validity of lessons learned from general world history.

Winning the war proved far more difficult and intractable than any high level official had ever imagined, except George Ball, an adviser quickly absorbed and discounted as the official in-house dissenter. There was no review of the basic decision to intervene. There were, however, constant reviews of the means being used to win, assuming the policy model continued to hold. As these means continued to fail, the decisionmakers searched for alternatives they believed would be marginal to the current ones and so acceptable to their internal constituencies. Although they would casually mention programs and actions suggested by the available alternatives—the Moderate or Radical Dove models—it was only for rejecting them in favor of their basic "Munich" model.

Secretary of Defense McNamara had become famous for his strong taste for analytic methods in the design and procurement of strategic nuclear and conventional force structure. However, he did not see fit to apply systems analysis to the strategy or conduct of the war. In his latest book on the war, he observes that he knew how to make cars, but did not know the history of Vietnam. He does not record any personal attempts at the time to inform himself about that history when the war began. So, to him, North Vietnam was a mere tool of the Chinese and the Soviet Union.

Many years after the war McNamara discovered intellectual "path dependence." Different national histories led to different "mind sets" over values and objectives. Consequently, there will always be inherent difficulty in achieving mutually satisfactory outcomes for the parties involved. McNamara, in his series of books on the war, never comes to grip with his own belief, expressed much earlier, in the worth of rational analysis in any kind of enterprise.

When, in 1967, McNamara finally decided to review the war, he chose a lengthy historical narrative. He did not commission the systems analysis techniques that he himself had pioneered in the Pentagon.[4] The so-called *Pentagon Papers* were a voluminous narrative history of the actual strategies pursued with some estimates of the effectiveness of the strategies. They did not present an evaluated set of alternatives that decisionmakers might consider. There was enough material in them to discover any kind of alternative and any kind of lesson.[5]

EVERYONE NEEDS AN *EX ANTE* POLICY MODEL

Now decisionmakers at any level of government have to construct, invent, or borrow some *ex ante* policy model. Even decisionmakers who are truly opportunistic, Machiavellian,

---

4. Many Dove authors attribute failures in Vietnam to systems analysis as the "soft" complement to a "technowar." However, the demand for formal systems analysis of the war fighting strategy was very slim. Alain Enthoven, the Assistant Secretary of Defense for Systems Analysis, used "back of the envelope" calculations to show that the North could sustain its rate of attrition indefinitely.

5. The *Pentagon Papers* left out important history and perspectives. There is little coverage of reporting systems. For example, the insatiable demand for numbers and other indicators that would show the United States was winning probably helped corrupt intelligence collection and analysis. Given a strategy of winning through attrition, and lack of geographic indicators of gain or loss, high body count became the indicator of success. Generals had incentives to use the tactics that appeared to produce this indicator, not necessarily the tactics most effective in defeating insurgents. They also had an incentive to inflate the count in every engagement. Body count, however, was not something brand new to the U.S. Army. Chinese entry into the Korean War turned it into a war of attrition, and so body count in Korea became a primary indicator. See Gartner and Myers (1995).

personal utility maximizers with no real interest in the public outcomes of their behavior must still offer up nominally connected substantive reasons for what they do. Their own bureaucracies, clients, constituents, and adversaries then accept and use these reasons in forming their own policy models. Policy models revealed strongly by top decisionmakers cascade through operating bureaucracies. At each level, the policy model of the moment serves as the claim for additional resources and influence. Such claims are not at all restricted to war or foreign policy. For example, if decisionmakers assert international trade competitiveness is a problem, then agencies remote from such a problem will assert that their programs clearly have a role to play in making the U.S. more competitive. If global warming is the problem, then all programs contribute to solving the global warming problem.

Now we can always evaluate current policy models by warning of some large, but plausible counterfactual swings from small variations in the reality on the ground. Sometimes those counterfactuals come packaged as the "lessons of history." Decisionmakers, currently using model M, are ignoring the relevant lessons learned from analogous historical situation X and should be using model N. Had they learned and applied what situation X teaches us before they acted, then the observed outcome produced by model N would be superior to the one that is really occurring. However, even if decisionmakers suddenly became willing to learn the lessons of history, these lessons are usually about means and have some circularity.

The core lessons of history loop back to the value components of the alternative model N from which the preferred lesson is extracted. Compare, for example, a Radical Dove such as Kolko (1985), who believes the war was misguided on moral grounds. Consequently, the lesson history teaches is that no nation ought to try to intervene and determine the historical path of some other nation. For Kolko, winning the war in Vietnam would have been evil. Immediate withdrawal would have been the practical advice he cared to give were he asked to give it. In contrast, if we believe the United States was morally correct in fighting the cold war, then the Vietnam War becomes necessary, even if lost. History tells us strong signals have to be sent to a malevolent adversary, in this case the then Soviet Union (Lind, 1999). By using a very costly signal, its willingness to inflict large amounts of pain on itself, the United States showed its will not to lose the cold war in the longer run and, maybe, to win it. And it did win. So for Lind, we have a validated lesson of history. Losing a war is messy, but fighting it may be necessary. For Lind, losing could be highly moral, since large scale resistance to local aggression helped destroy the Soviet Union's "evil empire." Stay in and invest some more would have been his advice had he been asked to provide some at the time. There will be payoff in the long run.

Now we have described an intellectual tragedy, because there are no criteria or rules for determining whose *ex ante* policy models will be adequate for their purpose. We judge their adequacy, in hindsight, after they have been tried. However, we know bad outcomes result from the best and most examined policy models that decisionmakers can construct. Conversely, good outcomes may result from some random process, even though the decisionmakers used some model that was prima facie logically invalid or empirically unsound.

Given that no policy model can ever really be verified in some scientific sense, there are roughly six basic ways to improve them. I have ordered them from simple-to-apply to complex-to-apply: (1) establish ad hoc criteria for checking that the internal structure of a model is logically consistent and transparent; (2) infer the correct lessons of history; (3) design a vigilant internal decision process to construct a model and check out its critical assumptions and pitfalls; (4) introduce external bureaucratic "competition" in the production of policy models; (5) improve the cognition of individual decisionmakers and help them avoid decision traps; and (6) create learning organizations that can learn quickly but correctly from experience and can pursue flexible policies in response to what it learns.

STANDARD CHECKLISTS OR QUESTIONS

Suppose constructing a policy model is like building a house. Good craft in building this house assures that the house will be livable and have the properties the owners specified when they authorized construction. Good and bad craft in house building can be tested by some inspector who roams around the house with a checklist or a code that lists the things minimally adequate houses must have. Similarly, applying check lists, questions, or codes for policy models may reveal the care and craft with which they were constructed (Hambrick,1974). If decisionmakers or their advisers have such devices, they can deconstruct their policy models into standard propositional types and check them to see if all the standard propositions have been stated (completeness test). Each proposition can then be reviewed for soundness if it is an empirical type or validity if it is a logical statement. The existence of good reasons can be checked with "ought" statements.

Consider the following checklist for the decisionmakers' model adopted from Hambrick:

1. *Value proposition*: The United States ought to deter direct or indirect Soviet and (Chinese) aggression in the Third World.

   1.1 *Auxiliary grounding proposition*: If the United States intervenes in Vietnam, then we will deter the Soviet Union from interventions in developing countries and show resolve in our larger confrontation.[6]

---

6. An alternative grounding proposition is that the mere act of intervening, whether successful or not, will accomplish some U.S. goals in the long run (Lind, 1999). If decisionmakers believe the latter kind of grounding proposition at the time they decide to intervene, then they can take comfort knowing that they only need to show or signal *sufficient* resistance, not win the conflict.

2. *Conditional policy action*: If the United States forecasts that an ally will be unable to contain or defeat communist insurgency, the United States must intervene to defeat the insurgency.

3. *Indirect consequence*: Intervention itself undermines local democracy.

4. *Constraints proposition*: Previous interventions have not been successful in this place at other times.

5. *Comparative cost-effectiveness*: Resources and forces must be sufficient and different enough in kind to overcome past constraints.

Given this deconstruction into standard propositions, we can observe whether the model corresponds to good craft or not. For example, craft says a "good" model should be "complete" but "parsimonious." The decisionmakers' model in Vietnam was "over-complete," since it contained so many reasons for staying in Vietnam and escalating. A good model should be able to confront a weak test of falsification or disverification. In Vietnam, it was very difficult to specify such a test.

Neustadt and May similarly claim that a checklist or template derived from routine, but competent foreign policy staff work will be helpful in sorting out policy models. Staff should have some knowledge of analogous historical events. For example, they suggest:

1. *Ask what, when, why questions about the specific history of an issue or problem*: Thus, U.S. decisionmakers might have studied the history of Vietnam back to 1945 or before for clues to a workable policy model.[7] They might have talked to the

---

7. March, Sproull, and Tamuz [1991(1996)], for example, talk about "near-histories," for example, the U.S. considered intervention in

substantive experts they employed or the historians of Vietnam on the outside.

2. *Identify the interests involved*: U.S. decisionmakers should have been at work sorting out the nation's interest in local democracy for developing nations from its interest in taking a stand to demonstrate willingness to fight the cold war.

3. *Construct historical similarities and differences*: When analogies carry heavy weight in some constructed policy model, write down the similarities and differences between the analogy and the current situation. Force the advocates to say what facts would change their minds.

4. *Test presumptions about the current course of action*: A challenge to a presumption is another way of saying construct some plausible counterfactuals that satisfy rules for an adequate lesson of history. For each challenge, they suggest force a "willingness to pay" question. Since uncertainty is always characteristic of policy models, Neustadt and May mean the adviser's willingness to pay expressed in terms of a hypothetical bet about the correctness of their advice. Decisionmakers should ask advisers to bet the budget of their own agency or their own salary on the worth the actions they are recommending. Advisers who lose such bets will, of course, never have to pay them. However, the bets are heuristics for eliciting the degree of confidence an adviser has in their story. Those who solicit such bets implicitly believe that their advisers do not engage in strategic behavior or lying to promote the acceptance of their own advice or agenda.

1954, but did not. And they talk about "hypothetical histories," counterfactual, but plausible narratives that vary sensitive parameters. See the section below on learning the lessons of history correctly.

LEARNING THE LESSONS OF
HISTORY CORRECTLY

Pure narrative historians have little use for policy applications of their craft, preferring instead to get their specific facts straight and complete. However, when asked, they frequently intuit lessons of history from some particular sample of one or two that they have been describing, even though they know, by trade and training, the world is full of contingencies and uncertainties. Any lesson based on a limited, but detailed example of one from the real world can have limited didactic power or even be highly misleading. Yet historians do not ordinarily say that their discipline is a form of private consumption, and not a form of intellectual investment or capital formation. By learning enough history, they believe, decisionmakers can learn to compare and contrast their current situation with those of the past, acquiring useful strategies and avoiding pitfalls that others have suffered.

For each *ex ante* policy model offered during the war, the chief method of "verification" was a projected alternative history, some counterfactual story and a set of policies and actions branching from the situation the decisionmakers had created. Each competing counterfactual policy said if only the decisionmakers would give up on their model and start following the military or Dove prescriptions, outcomes would turn out to be much better.

Counterfactual arguments appear all the time in social science, when different hypothetical causes can be "controlled." Applied policy science tries to invent counterfactuals for decisionmakers to implement. For example, in statistical policy models with policy instruments as well-specified independent variables, varying the value of some instruments from their current or their average values is automatically a counterfactual. For example, quantitative economic historians claim they can "control" the causes that affected the historical demand or supply of commodities sold in some market where transactions have been recorded. By varying some theoretically persuasive independent variable, they then can show what would have happened in some market, all other things being held equal statistically. If some independent variable turns out to be a policy or instrumental variable that historical decisionmakers could have controlled, then so much the better. However, statistical policy models come with specification, significance, and power tests.

Ordinarily, international relations experts cannot construct statistical models useful to diplomats or decisionmakers. Yet the former want their work to be useful to the latter. As a partial substitute for model building, international relations policy analysts construct sets of plausible rules hoping to give counterfactual advice and arguments the same standing that statistical social science models have. They want to deliver persuasive and actionable lessons of history.[8] Assume that the people offering the lessons of history are sincere and not engaged in strategic manipulation to obtain personal or organizational objectives. Then how do we judge advice deduced from historical cases and examples?

When we use statistical policy models, we check the plausibility of the specification and the statistical significance of the coefficients, individually and collectively. We assume that an increase or decrease in the value of some instrumental variable will induce some desired policy behavior. People, cities, states, or nations will start doing things or stop doing things, depending on the level of aggregation in the model.[9] Sophisticated analysts check

---

8. See the papers in Tetlock and Belkin (1996) on proposed rules for constructing plausible counterfactuals. See the simplified rules offered in Jentleman (2000).

9. Social scientists, unlike many economists, believe that the actors affected by some policy do not have rational expectations and good information. They do not act to change the structure of the decisionmakers' model so as to defeat policy actions. Pure rational expectations economists hold that no policy can be effective unless decisionmakers surprise everyone, because the set of known and unknown actors subject to the policy will negate it if they have the time.

for effect size as well, since it makes little sense to invest economic or political capital in changes that appear statistically significant, but have only small impact.

To draw lessons from a particular case, historians and policy analysts attempt to change one "variable" at a time in the case while holding context and the other independent variables as close to constant as plausibility allows. Counterfactual scenarios can be fanciful and extended, so analysts have tried to set boundary conditions on their credibility. For example, Jentleson (2000) holds that counterfactual scenarios can be used to show how a "preventive" diplomacy option can be useful to diplomats and decision-makers considering intervention in low level international crisis or war. Paraphrasing Jentleson's five rules for constructing counterfactuals, we have:

1   *Specificity*: There must exist some feasible action or instrument that could make a difference in the path an actual event took.

2. *Minimal historical rewrite*: There should be minimal divergence from the actual historical path: Minimal historical rewrite is equivalent to holding all variables but one constant in some statistically constructed policy model.

3. *Plausible causal logic*: Once some single change has been made, and letting rules (1) and (2) hold, there must be evidence drawn from some source of validated knowledge that lets the path be different and desirable. That body of knowledge has to exist prior to the counterfactual being constructed and be exogenous. It can be drawn from diplomatic theory, game theory, theory of economic sanctions, etc.[10]

---

10. There are no subrules on how many bodies of knowledge may be used to provide the needed causal logic. Counterfactual designers can keep adding bodies of knowledge so that collectively they warrant the

4. *No hindsight: Knowledge available to the decisionmaker at the time of decision*: Assuming that conditions (1)-(3) can be satisfied, then that they could hold must be known at the time decisionmakers took their real world historical action.

5. *Feasibility*: Assuming conditions (1)-(4) hold, decisionmakers could actually have taken some alternative action than the one they did take, and it will be bounded if they do take it.[11]

Any usable counterfactual must assume away the "butterfly" effects conjured by complexity theory. Small variations in policy never have massive unpredictable consequences and spillovers, and large variations never have small or zero consequences. The counterfactual historical world conjured up by some alternative policy action is not too different than the one with which we start and really predictable, and it can work if tried. So decisionmakers can take an alternative course arguably more effective than the current one. Each counterfactual variation in current policy suggested as an improvement has just the *right size* consequences to establish the projected result desired. Thus, preventive diplomacy to prevent ethnic cleansing in the Balkans does not escalate into a major war. If the counterfactual policy being advocated, had identifiable butterfly effects, it would never be tendered. The projected consequences would always be too large or too small.

Suppose then that rules (1)-(5) for proper counterfactuals all hold. If these establish the surface plausibility and the feasibility of some alternative, then an action recommendation still requires a missing rule (6):

---

counterfactual action being proposed.

11. Jentleson follows Tetlock and Belkin (1996, p. 18), but he tries to simplify. Tetlock and Belkin present six criteria: (1) clarity; (2) logical consistency; (3) minimal rewrite; (4) theoretical consistency (existence of some validated knowledge base); (5) statistical consistency; (6) projectability into some possible, but plausible world.

6. *Cost*: The perceived economic and social costs of the counterfactual alternative must be low enough to induce the counterfactual suggested. Even the right size action may be very costly to implement. Furthermore, the preferred counterfactual policy must permit some flexibility in case it proves wrong. Advice based on proper counterfactual constructions can still be wrong advice. So we need a rule (7).

7. *Flexibility*: Assuming that rules (1)-(6) hold, then the counterfactual is preferred that permits decisionmakers opportunity to adjust the counterfactual. For example, the United States and NATO decisionmakers initially believed that a small dose of high altitude bombing would induce Serbia to leave Kosovo, but it took a high dose over a long period of time. However, the number of aircraft and the sorties they flew could easily be stepped up when the initial forecast about the adversary's response proved wrong.[12]

Suppose that the Kennedy-Johnson decisionmakers directed analysts to do some counterfactual scenarios at the critical periods of the war that we have reviewed, 1961, 1965, and 1968. Could these analysts have produced some counterfactual policies that met rules (1)-(7)? Assume that our decisionmakers were ordinary, bounded rationality decisionmakers with cognitive decision biases with much routine business to transact. Assume that they were running ordinary bureaucracies with their standard routines for finding and implementing alternatives.

---

12. History tells us some nations quit when exposed to sufficiently high levels of force as Serbs did in their response to the intense NATO bombing in Kosovo in 1999. Some nations when exposed to mere threats or low levels of force decide to negotiate. *Ex ante*, no one can really predict who will do what. Persuading decisionmakers to pursue an alternative is the aim of counterfactual models rather than accurate prediction.

Advocates construct counterfactual policy models to show how their preferred values can be accomplished. So, the military could claim the counterfactual: larger scale, less-controlled military force would lead to "success." Simultaneously, Doves could argue that being more controlled would lead to "success." Their definitions of success differed. Success for the military was destroying the enemy. The counterfactual policy action they wanted was authorization to destroy the enemy faster anywhere. Success for the Doves was a negotiated settlement with the adversary, never mind whether the settlement was honorable. Honor was a construction of some privileged elite anyway. The definition of success was not dependent on any positive or negative impact on the larger cold war. To Doves, the cold war was primarily a product of paranoia and communication failures by U.S. decisionmakers and not worth fighting even if real.

If we allow competing values in as part of a counterfactual, then it seems possible to construct competing policy models that would meet the seven rules for good counterfactuals I have constructed above. Under our assumption of boundedly rational decisionmakers and self-promoting bureaucracies, it seems very likely efforts to discriminate these competing counterfactuals would be limited, and decisionmakers would keep using their initial policy model. Since all parties could conform to the seven rules for constructing valid counterfactuals, asking for a choice was equivalent to asking for a choice among competing values. The designers of counterfactuals have no way of demonstrating that competing values can be ordered and compared persuasively. I conclude that learning the lessons of history through properly constructed counterfactual policy models would not have helped the decisionmakers we had.

An Internal Marketplace
of Ideas

Instead of subjecting some single *ex ante* policy model to review, decisionmakers can construct their models by a process of intellectual competition and multiple advocacy. The stakeholders are allowed to advocate their own models within the framework of an implicit competitive market that evaluates their worth and sets up rates of "exchange." An "equilibrium," synthesized model then emerges that contains the most cost-effective and consistent policies for central decisionmakers to pursue.

Intellectual competition is the solution proposed by Alexander George (1972, 1980). George argues for multiple advocacy—a system designed to encourage advice that produces alternative, and even opposing, positions. George uses many of the same historical cases as the "lessons of history" writers to identify "malfunctions" of the presidential decisionmaking process: for example, when advisers reach agreement too quickly, when the president is dependent on a single source of information, or when advisers see a problem, but are unwilling to alert the president to it. Such malfunctions can occur in bureaucratic advisory groups or informal ones. They are to be minimized by using more than one set of advisers.

Assuming there is no failure in this predesigned marketplace of ideas, then the bureaucratized competition forces one to be vigilant as the manager of the competition. However, like markets for goods or services, the marketplace of ideas may "fail." It clearly has high coordination costs, and intense competition may just install even firmer beliefs about the utility of one's own models. Unless this idea market has good "auctioneers" able to keep control of the "prices" offered and accepted, multiple advocacy modes may be high cost and not information-revealing. If decisionmakers are not well informed, competition will by itself not be sufficient. Untangling competing advice, each piece of advice surrounded by a net of supporting assumptions and facts, requires competition *and* very skeptical decisionmakers (Milgrom and Roberts, 1986).

IMPROVING THE DECISIONMAKERS

We can always use better trained, better informed, flexible decisionmakers in any kind of policy situation. *Ex post*, Secretary McNamara and the other principals report that the U.S. decisionmakers did not know Vietnamese history, did not know the mind-set of the enemy or the putative ally, and never considered direct contact with the North Vietnamese decisionmakers as an alternative to sending ambiguous signals through an easily mis-interpreted large scale military campaign.[13] Gathering strategic intelligence on an adversary and checking that the adversary is receiving the signals I send correctly seems elementary and prudential in the conduct of war. The puzzle is why did the principals not do these things. There are two answers. First, their desires for information and their action preferences may suffer from individual psychological biases. Second, even if they were individually making calculations correctly, some flaw existed in their collective decision making.

Decision psychologists have produced a very large number of theories and experiments about judgment and actual decision making.[14] The experiments, however, generally involve subjects who are not practicing, high level decisionmakers or bureaucrats. For example, Arkes and Blumer (2000) believe that paying attention to sunk cost is a robust judgment error, whereas any accomplished bureaucrat knows that sunk costs are very important to the future of their unit and that they are ignored at some peril to one's self and one's agency. The decision and judgment literature by psychologists do not really address political and bureaucratic

---

13. McNamara et al. (1999), *op. cit.*, pp. 392-393.
14. See, for example, the 40 articles in Connolly, Arkes, and Hammond (2000).

calculus. So they find judgment errors when decisionmakers act to complete bad projects discovered to be bad and do not make proper calculations at the margin about the benefits of new outlays.

Prospect theory holds that individuals have certain decision biases when considering marginal benefits and marginal costs or losses taken from some arbitrary zero point (Kahneman and Tversky, 2000). The heuristics may create bad outcomes from the standpoint of some objective observer. If people, for example, are poor, but risk prone in the face of some net losses, then they may send good money after bad, because of their psychology of loss. They do not think about sunk costs "correctly" and so suffer a real decline in their welfare (Arkes and Blumer, 2000). Racing to recover sunk costs and taking high risks to do so, of course, is a highly rational strategy by bureaucrats, because if they ignore them, their organizational welfare in the form of budget and personnel will clearly decline (Averch, 1990). Sunk costs in the form of visibly unfinished, but now known to be cost-ineffective projects are highly costly to an agency's long run welfare, no matter that decision theory and economics advise they should be ignored.

Prospect theory, a particular variant of individual judgment and decision theories, has had perhaps the most appeal to students of war and international relations. Prospect theory holds that all human decision making is flawed, because people use heuristics and short cuts in attacking problems.[15] These heuristics are pervasive in foreign conflict situations full of risk and uncertainty,

---

15. See Kahneman and Tversky (1979, 1984) for the original exposition. They report that the way people actually make decisions is different than the way normative theories say they should be made. There is a lengthy quarrel between the descriptive prospect theory and normative utility theory found in economics and decision science. Prospect theory has not yet converted the economics and management and decision science professions from insisting that rational people should be maximizing expected utility or expected profit or some objective function.

perhaps, because we can write stories about actual decisionmaking we can make conform to prospect theory. Assuming (1) most presidents can act like a solitary, unitary decisionmakers, perhaps after synthesizing and integrating all the information they get from their bureaucracies, (2) and that their bureaucracies actually do what they say, and (3) there are no surprises or unexpected events, McDermott (1998) attempts to show that prospect theory extends across administrations and administrators of very different character.

She, for example, treats President Carter's decision making in the abortive Iranian hostage crisis of 1979 and his decision to admit the Shah of Iran to the United States as two historical failures based on prospect theory. Then she treats Eisenhower's U-2 crisis in 1960, another failure, and the 1956 Suez Crisis, a failure in the deterrence of allies and a success in *ex post* coercion.

It is likely that one can interpret any crisis or foreign policy decision in terms of prospect theory or of its chief competitor, expected utility theory, since the connectivity between the historical evidence and the theory being tested is always weak. If one wants to believe in prospect theory, then one can construct evidence for it from the historical record. If one wants to believe that presidents are expected maximizers of national interests, and just look at the world differently than prospect theorists, one can construct a story to this effect.

In a nutshell, prospect theory holds for individuals, there exists a highly specific "value" function that is concave in gains and convex in losses. Value is defined from some zero base or point of origin. Such a shape implies behavior to conserve positive values or gains and to avoid taking risky actions. In the case of losses, the value function implies risk prone behavior, because a decision-maker can reduce losses by risky actions, and if they do not pan out there is little additional loss that will be incurred. The value function is weighted not by "normal," subjective probability weights, but by a "decision weight" function that gives greater psychological weight to unlikely events and lower psychological weight to highly likely events. So if one maximizes the value function weighted by the psychological weighting function, then one can get behavior significantly at variance with expected utility theory. Since the value function is centered on some psychological zero point (no perceived gain or loss), then the "framing" of the problem or the crisis becomes all important. Vietnam decision-makers by their own testimony were likely to select the wrong frame—McNamara thought the North Vietnamese were Chinese agents. However, it probably does not take judgment biases projected by prospect theory to produce an erroneous framing of a decision. Frame conflicts are inherent in any political process independent of individual judgmental biases.[16]

Now my interest in prospect theory is whether it can be used in evaluating policy models and improving them. If real decisionmakers knew they were all prisoners of psychological heuristics and behaved according to prospect theory, would we produce better policy models and better decisions than we would using ordinary checklists, the lessons of history, counterfactual policy models or advisory competitions.

If one wants to use prospect theory to assist decisionmakers and not to infer their behavior, then the theory needs to be converted to a check list of do's or don'ts or into a list for avoiding decision traps. For example, Russo and Schoemaker (1989) propose 10 rules derived from prospect theory for creating an excellent decision process. As we would expect, most of the rules go to the construction of frames (the zero point in the value function). It is difficult to provide general prescriptions for reconstructing value (utility) functions to have the proper shape, the concavities and convexities, over the gains and losses for a

---

16. Schön and Rein (1994) argue for policy analysis as techniques for resolving frame conflicts in the presence of intractable policy controversies. For them, once frame conflicts have been resolved through dialogue, the preferred alternatives become clear, and their choice becomes a matter of costs and benefits.

particular situation.[17] They list plunging in without thinking about the frame; frame blindness—solving the wrong problem; over reliance on rules of thumb; not reweighting probabilities in the light of new evidence; winging it. They argue, like most decision theorists, that their preferred decision process cannot guarantee a good outcome, but that it may help avoid bad outcomes.

Assume then that we have converted the originally descriptive prospect theory into prescriptive behavior and behavior avoidance. Given that we had no monolithic, dictatorial decisionmaker in Vietnam, suppose the counterfactual that we had a set of decision-makers in Vietnam who used these prescriptions. Would the operational policy models have been any better or more carefully searched? Would anyone have suggested that the United States undertake direct communications with the Vietnamese to do our signaling rather than undertaking "bomb and pause" as the preferred signals?

Since bad outcomes for individuals result from behaving according to prospect theory, we can derive a set of self-reflective rules for reconsidering our frames and our behavior toward risk. *However, the decisionmaking over Vietnam was one of value functions, zero points, and probabilities in conflict.* So even if everyone followed the rules for avoiding their own decision traps, there is no guarantee that there could have been be some correct aggregate value function and frame for the United States decisionmaking in Vietnam. We can certainly say that good individual judgment is a necessary condition for a good outcome in Vietnam or for any problem. However, there is no invisible hand here that forces these good judgments into some coherent aggregate. So we are then led to theories of organizational decisionmaking.

---

17. Some successful businessmen, for example, are risk prone, "bet the company" people, even when they are in the gain part of their value function, because they believe they can change the height and shape of their value function.

VIGILANT DECISION PROCESSES

Janis (1989) is associated with the notion of a "vigilant" internal decision process on important problems confronting an organization. A vigilant decision process is an optimal search for an optimal solution to a problem. For important classes of problems, Janis urges "vigilant," but not "hypervigilant" problem solving. In a vigilant state, the decisionmaker essentially forces himself to produce the information both necessary and sufficient for a high quality decision, despite any cognitive difficulties he may have and despite any bureaucratic pathologies his organization may have. In fact, a high quality decision is exactly the one revealed by a vigilant process.

The steps in a vigilant decision making process are: (1) appraise the challenge of decisionmaking proactively; (2) conduct a thorough self-analysis and an organizational analysis using both subjective and objective knowledge; (3) survey the alternatives by considering a wide range of alternative courses of action and stay open; (4) evaluate the alternatives by finding new information; (5) take account of any new information, even when it does not support the course of action initially preferred; (5) carefully project and weigh both positive and negative consequences of each alternative; (6) determine the optimal course of action; (7) include contingency plans in risky situations.

In appraising vigilant decision processes, there are questions of benefit and of cost. On the benefit side, if we are going to be vigilant, we have to assume a policy model constructed through some such process can shift the distribution of outcomes toward those that are more preferred rather than less. Hammond (1996) argues that in really uncertain worlds, good outcomes, even from the best decision process, can only be probabilistic. He implies that some combination of intuition and empirical research can let one estimate the distribution of outcomes.

Then there is a question of cost. Since public decisionmakers are always short of time and attention, and commonly face strategic behavior by their agents and constituents, constructing a vigilant decision process may be too costly. Some psychologists hold that heuristics and short cuts used in ordinary, non-vigilant decision processes produce about as good an actual outcome. See Suedfeld and Tetlock (1992).

LEARNING ORGANIZATIONS

Among management scientists, creating learning organizations has been much in vogue, since Senge (1990) popularized them. How organizations learn and survive when they are staffed by people with individual decision biases is surprisingly not a problem addressed intensely either by decision psychologists or by learning organization theorists. See Cavaleri and Fearon (1996) and Shapira (1997). Senge et al. (1999) present a whole series of exercises and cases for decisionmakers on how to create learning organizations with no reference to the biases in individual judgment found by psychologists and the strategic behavior discussed by game theorists.

WHERE DO WE STAND NOW?

All of these methods for constructing adequate policy models suggest that decisionmakers need to become more self-aware and more self-critical of the kind of activity they engage in when making policy or giving advice. Even if they gain this consciousness, there are still no formal tests for choosing one policy model over another. Nor does "policy science" promise such tests very soon. To the extent that models contain competing empirical statements, they should be tested. It seems possible to check even the macropolitical statements about the behavior of nation-states that decisionmakers commonly use. Furthermore, if actions rest on predictions, then the predictions should be recorded and, at least, have implicit probability weights assigned. Those who consistently make good predictions can then be defined as having "informed judgment," and their judgments can be drawn upon extensively.

Nevertheless, unless some effort is made to draw out the data the adviser uses in his predictions and check it out with other data, policymaking will remain mysterious.

Everyone's model must be open to criticism, and decision-makers should examine the criticism as objectively as possible. Yet the implicit organizational dilemma for such criticism is that it is unlikely the criticism will be taken seriously if coupled with political opposition. The fate of the Dove models clearly shows this. One possible locus for such criticism is the congress, but within our governmental structure, congressional criticism—at least in the form of alternative models and policies—necessarily is political opposition.

Different kinds of advice giving are needed for different kinds of situations and different kinds of administrations. Eisenhower's National Security Council did not work for Kennedy; Kennedy's did not work for Johnson, nor Johnson's for Nixon. No prespecified policy ombudsman seems likely to be universally appropriate. Yet informed skepticism, the persistent and deliberate questioning of models, is needed. Depending upon the tastes of particular presidents and the structures of different administrations, such advocates and staff might be located in various places in the Departments of State or Defense. Perhaps the White House itself is an alternative locus for such institutionalized skepticism. However, any White House staff will always remain committed to the current president, and must be dedicated to implementing their current policy. Such positioning might discourage what is needed.[18]

The intellectual problem revealed by the Vietnam War remains unsolved a quarter of a century later. Perhaps it is significant that

---

18. Proposals arise from time to time to arm the presidency with a general policy analysis capability, but no president has ever seen fit to set one up. The Congress has provided the president with a built in capability for science and technology advice through the Office of Science and Technology Policy and its dual head, the resident personal science adviser.

the people who won the war had a rigorous system of self-criticism at all organizational levels and through organized self-criticism learned to cope with the United States

BIBLIOGRAPHY

Adams, S. (1994). *War of Numbers: An Intelligence Memoir*. South Royalston, VT: Steerforth Press.

Almond, G., and Verba, S. (1963). *The Civic Culture: Political Attitudes and Democracy in Five Nations*. Princeton, NJ: Princeton University Press.

An, T. S. (1998). *The Vietnam War*. Madison, NJ: Fairleigh Dickinson University Press.

Arkes, H. R., and Blumer, C. (2000). The Psychology of Sunk Cost. In T. Connolly, H. R. Arkes, and K. R. Hammond (Eds.), *Judgment and Decision Making: An Interdisciplinary Reader* (2nd ed.) (pp. 97-113). Cambridge, UK: Cambridge University Press.

Averch, H. (1990). *Private Markets and Public Intervention*. Pittsburgh, PA: University of Pittsburgh Press.

Ball, G. (1982). *The Past has Another Pattern*. New York: W. W. Norton & Company.

Ball, M. A. (1992). *Vietnam-On-The-Potomac*. New York: Praeger.

Baron, J. (1998). *Intuition and Error in Public Decision Making*. New York: Oxford University Press.

Barrett, D. M. (1993). *Uncertain Warriors: Lyndon Johnson and His Vietnam Advisers*. Lawrence, KA: University Press of Kansas.

Barret, D. M. (2000). The Mythology Surrounding Lyndon Johnson, His Advisers and the 1965 Decision to Escalate the Vietnam War. In W. L. Hixon (Ed.), *Leadership and Diplomacy in the Vietnam War* (pp. 17-44). New York: Garland Publishing, Inc.

Barrett, D. M. (Ed.). (1997). *Lyndon B. Johnson's Vietnam Papers: A Documentary Collection*. College Station, TX: Texas A&M Press.

BDM Corporation. (1979a). *A Study of Strategic Lessons Learned in Viet Nam: Volume 1. The Enemy.* (BDM/W-78-128-R). McLean, VA: BDM Corporation.

BDM Corporation. (1979b). *A Study of Strategic Lessons Learned in Viet Nam, Volume II, South Vietnam.* (BDM/W-78-128-TR). McLean, VA: BDM Corporation.

Bennet, C. J. (1991). How States Utilize Foreign Evidence. *Journal of Public Policy, 11,* 31-54.

Bennet, C. J., and Howlett, M. H. (1992). The Lessons of learning: Reconciling Theories of Policy Learning and Policy Change. *Policy Sciences, 25,* 275-294.

Bergen, J. D. (1986). *U.S. Army Vietnam: Military Communications: A Test for Technology.* Washington, DC. Center of Military History, U.S. Army

Berman, L. (1982). *Planning a Tragedy.* New York: W. W. Norton.

Bernstein, I. (1996). *Guns or Butter: The Presidency of Lyndon Johnson.* New York: Oxford University Press.

Betts, R. K. (1977). *Soldiers, Statesman, and Cold War Scholars.* Cambridge, MA: Harvard University Press.

Blight, J. G., and Welch, D. A. (1990). *On the Brink: Americans and Soviets Reexamine the Cuban Missile Crisis* (2nd Ed.). New York: Hill and Wang.

Bose, M. (1998). *Shaping and Signaling Presidential Policy: The National Security Decision Making of Eisenhower and Kennedy.* College Station, TX: Texas A&M University Press.

Bottone, S. (1965). There is No Lesser Evil in Vietnam. *New Politics, IV*(2), 5-17.

Braestrup, P. (Ed.). (1984). *Vietnam as History: Ten Years after the Paris Peace Accords.* Lanham, MD: University Press of America.

Breslauer, G. W., and Tetlock, P. E. (Eds). (1991). *Learning in U.S. and Soviet Foreign Policy.* Boulder, CO: Westview Press.

Brockner, J. (1992). The Escalation of Commitment to a Failing Course of Action: Toward Theoretical Progress. *Academy of Management Review, 17,* 39-61.

Brodie, F. M. (1981). *Richard Nixon: The Shaping of His Character.* New York: W. W. Norton.

Bundy, W. P. (1967). The Path to Vietnam: Ten Decisions, *Orbis, 11,* 647-663.

Burke, J. P., and Greenstein, F. I. (1989). *How Presidents Test Reality: Decisions on Vietnam, 1954 and 1965*. New York: Russell Sage.

Buzzanco, R. (1997). *Masters of War: Military Dissent and the Politics of the Vietnam Era*. Cambridge, UK: Cambridge University Press.

Cable, L. (1991). *Unholy Grail: The US and the Wars in Vietnam, 1965-1968*. New York: Routledge.

Calvert, R. L. (1985). The Value of Biased Information: A Rational Choice Model of Political Advice. *Journal of Politics, 47*, 531-55.

Cavaleri, S., and. Fearon, D. (Eds.). (1996). *Managing in Organizations that Learn*. Cambridge, MA: Blackwell.

Cerami, J. R. (2000). Presidential Decisionmaking and Vietnam: Lessons for Strategists. In W. L. Hixon (Ed.), *Leadership and Diplomacy in the Vietnam War* (pp. 224-238). New York: Garland Publishing, Inc.

Chomsky, N. (1969). *American Power and the New Mandarins*. New York: Vintage Books.

Chomsky, N. (1982, November). The Lessons of the Vietnam War. *Indochina Newsletter*, 1-5.

Chomsky, N. (1993). *Rethinking Camelot: JFK, the Vietnam War, and U.S. Political Culture*. Boston, MA: South End Press.

Clodfelter, M. (1989). *The Limits of Air Power: The American Bombing of North Vietnam*. New York: Free Press.

Cobb, R. W. (1973). The Belief Systems Perspective: An Assessment of a Framework. *Journal of Politics, 35*, 121-153.

Cobb, W. W., Jr. (1998). *The American Foundation Myth in Vietnam: Reigning Paradigms and Raining Bombs*. Lanham, MD: University Press of America.

Cohen, M. D., and Sproull, L. S. (Eds.). (1996). *Organizational Learning*. Thousand Oaks, CA: Sage Publications.

Colby, W. (1989). *Lost Victory: A First-hand Account of America's Sixteen Year Involvement in Vietnam*. Chicago, IL: Contemporary Books.

Colby, W., and Forbath, P. F. (1978). *Honorable Men: My Life in the CIA*. New York: Simon and Schuster.

Connolly, T., Arkes, H. R., and Hammond, K. R. (Eds.). (2000). *Judgment and Decision Making: An Interdisciplinary Reader* (2nd Ed.). Cambridge, UK: Cambridge University Press.

Cooper, C. (1970). *The Lost Crusade*. New York: Dodd, Mead.

Corson, W. R. (1974). *Consequences of Failure.* New York: W.W. Norton.

Currey, C. B. (1976). *The Craft and Crafting of History.* Sarasota, Fl: Omni Press.

Currey, C. B. (1981). *Self-Destruction: The Disintegration and Decay of the United States Army.* New York: W. W. Norton.

Currey, C. B. (1997). *Victory At Any Cost: The Genius of Viet Nam's Gen. Vo Nguyen Giap.* Washington, DC: Brassey's, Inc.

Dallek, R. (1991). *Lone Star Rising: Lyndon Johnson and His Times, 1908-1960.* New York: Oxford University Press.

Davidson, P. (1988). *Vietnam at War: The History, 1946-1975.* New York,: Oxford University Press.

Dean, V. M. (1962). Southeast Asia and Japan. In J. Roosevelt (Ed.), *The Liberal Papers* (253-270). Garden City, NY: Doubleday.

DeBenedetti, C. (1990). *An American Ordeal: The Antiwar Movement of the Vietnam Era.* Syracuse, NY: Syracuse University Press.

DeGroot, G. J. (2000). *A Noble Cause? America and the Vietnam War.* New York: Longman.

Demandt, A. (1993). *History That Never Happened: A Treatise on What Would Have Happened If...?* Jefferson, NC: McFarland & Company Publishers.

Drummond, H. (1996). *Escalation in Decision-Making: The Tragedy of Taurus.* New York: Oxford University Press.

Eidenburg, E. (1969). The Presidency: Americanizing the War in Vietnam. In A. P. Sindler (Ed.), *American Political Institutions and Public Policy* (pp. 68-126). Boston, MA: Little Brown and Company.

Ellsberg, D. (1970, January). Revolutionary Judo: Working Notes on Vietnam No. 10. Unpublished manuscript, D-19807-ARPA/Agile. Santa Monica, CA: The RAND Corporation.

Ellsberg, D. (1970, September). Escalating in a Quagmire. Paper presented at the annual meeting of the American Political Science Association. Los Angeles. CA.

Emerson, G. (1976). *Winners and Losers: Battles, Retreats, Gains, Losses and Ruins fro a Long War.* New York: Random House.

Enthoven, A. C., and Smith, W. K. (1971). *How Much is Enough: Shaping the Defense Program, 1961-1969.* New York: Harper and Row.

Etzioni, A. (1962). *The Hard Way to Peace: A New Strategy* (1st Ed.). Collier Books.

Ewell, J. and Hunt, I. A. (1974). *Sharpening the Combat Edge: The Use of Analysis to Reinforce Military Judgment.* Washington, DC: Department of the Army.

Fearon, J. D. (1991). Counterfactuals and Hypothesis Testing in Political Science. *World Politics, 43*(2), 169-95.

Fearon, J. D. (1994). Signaling Versus the Balance of Power and Interests: An Empirical Test of a Crisis Bargaining Model. *Journal of Conflict Resolution, 38*(2), 236-69.

Fearon, J. D. (1996). Causes and Counterfactuals in Social Science: Exploring an Analogy between Cellular Automata and Historical Processes. In P. E. Tetlock and Belkin, A. (Eds.), *Counterfactual Thought Experiments in World Politics: Logical, Methodological, and Psychological Perspectives* (pp. 39-67). Princeton, NJ: Princeton University Press.

Fischer, D. H. (1970). *Historians Fallacies: Toward a Logic of Historical Thought.* New York: Harper and Row.

FitzGerald, F. (1972). *Fire in the Lake: The Vietnamese and the Americans in Vietnam* Boston, MA: Little Brown.

Fogel, R. W. (1970). Historiography and Retrospective Econometrics. *History and Theory, IX*(3), 245-259.

Ford, H. P. (1998). *CIA and the Vietnam Policymakers : Three Episodes, 1962-1968.* Langley, VA: Center for the Study of Intelligence, CIA.

Fruchter, N. (1965). Statement on Vietnam. *Partisan Review*, 32, 624-627.

Gardner, L. C. (1988). *Approaching Vietnam: From World War II through Dienbienphu, 1941.* New York: W. W. Norton & Company.

Gardner, L. C. (1995). *Pay Any Price: Lyndon Johnson and the Wars for Vietnam.* Chicago, IL: Ivan R. Dee.

Gardner, L. C., and Gittinger, T. E. (1997). *Vietnam: The Early Decisions* (1st University of Texas ed.). Austin, TX: University of Texas Press.

Garfinkel, M. R. (2000). Conflict without Misperceptions or Incomplete Information. *Journal of Conflict Resolution, 44*(6), 793-807.

Garret, S. A. (1968). *An Intellectual Analysis of Foreign Policy Arguments: The Vietnam Debate.* Charlottesville. VA: University of Virginia.

Garret, S. A. (1978). *Ideals and Reality: An Analysis of the Debate Over Vietnam.* Washington, DC: University Press of America.

Garrison, J. A. (1999). *Games Advisors Play.* College Station, TX: Texas A&M University Press.

Gartner, S. A., and Myers, M. E. (1995). Body Counts and "Success" in the Vietnam and Korean Wars. *Journal of Interdisciplinary History, XXV,* 377-396.

Gavin, J. M, Gen. (1966, February). A Communication on Vietnam. *Harper's,* 16-17.

Geddes, B. (1990). How the Cases You Choose Affect the Answers You Get: Selection Bias in Comparative Politics. *Political Analysis, 8,* 131-50.

Gelb, L. H. (1970, September). Vietnam: The System Worked. Paper presented at the annual meeting of the American Political Science Association. Los Angeles, CA.

Gelb, L. H., and Betts, R. K. (1979). *The Irony of Vietnam: The System Worked.* Washington, DC: Brookings Institution.

George, A. L. (1972). The Case for Multiple Advocacy in Making Foreign Policy. *American Political Science Review, 66,* 751-785.

George, A. L. (1980). *Presidential Decision Making in Foreign Policy: The Effective Use of Information and Advice.* Boulder, CO: Westview Press.

Geva, N., and Mintz, A. (Eds.). (1997). *Decision Making in War and Peace: The Cognitive-Rational Debate.* Boulder, CO: Lynne Reinner.

Gibson, J. W. (1988). The Perfect War: The War We Couldn' t Lose and Didn't Win. New York: Atlantic Monthly Press.

Goodman, A. E. (1978). *The Lost Peace: America's Search for a Negotiated Settlement of the Vietnam War.* Stanford, CA: Hoover Institution Press.

Goodwin, R. N. (1966). *Triumph or Tragedy: Reflections on Vietnam.* New York: Alfred A. Knopf, Inc.

Graff, H. F. (1970). *The Tuesday Cabinet: Deliberation and Decisions on Peace and War under Lyndon B. Johnson.* Englewood Cliffs, NJ: Prentice Hall.

Halberstam, D. (1965). *The Making of a Quagmire.* New York: Random House.

Halberstam, D. (1969, July). The Very Expensive Education of McGeorge Bundy. *Harper's, 239*, 21-40.

Halberstam, D. (1971, February). The Programming of Robert McNamara. *Harper's, 242*, 37-71.

Halberstam, D. (1972). *The Best and the Brightest.* New York: Random House.

Hall, P. (1993). Policy Paradigms, Social Learning, and the State. *Comparative Politics, 25*, 275-296.

Halperin, M. H. (1963). *Limited War in the Nuclear* Age. New York: Wiley.

Hambrick, R. S., Jr. (1974). A Guide for the Analysis of Policy Analysis Arguments. *Policy Sciences, 5*, 469-478.

Hammer, E. J. (1987). *A Death in November: America in Vietnam, 1963.* New York: E. P. Dutton.

Hammond, K. R. (1996). *Human Judgment and Social Policy: Irreducible Uncertainty, Inevitable Error, Unavoidable Injustice.* New York: Oxford University Press.

Hammond, J. S., Keeney, R. L., and Raiffa, H. (1999). *Smart Choices: A Practical Guide to Making Better Decisions.* Boston, MA: Harvard Business School Press.

Harris, W. H. (1965, September 28). Morality, Moralism, and Vietnam. *Christian Century, 83*, 1151-1157.

Harvey, F. P. and Mor, B. D. (Eds.). (1998). *Advances in the Study of Crisis, War, and Peace.* New York: St. Martin's Press.

Hatcher, P. L. (1990). *The Suicide of an Elite: American Internationalists and Vietnam.* Stanford, CA: Stanford University

Head, W. E., and Grinter, L. E. (Eds.). (1993). *Looking Back on the Vietnam War: A 1990's Perspective on the Decisions, Combat and Legacies.* Westport, CT.

Hemmer, C. M. (1998). Which Lessons Matter? Domestic Analogies, Analogical Choice and United States Foreign Policy. Unpublished doctoral dissertation, Cornell University.

Henderson, W. D. (1979). *Why the Vietcong Fought: A Study of Motivations and Control in the Modern Army in Combat.* Westport, CT: Greenwood Press.

Herek, G. M. (1987). Decision Making during International Crises: Is Quality of Process Related to Outcomes. *Journal of Conflict Resolution, 31,* 203-226.

Herring, G. C. (1985). *America's Longest War: The United States and Vietnam: 1950-1975.* New York: Alfred Knopf.

Herring, G. C. (1993a). The Johnson Administration's Conduct of a Limited War in Vietnam. In W. Head and L. E. Grinter (Eds.), *Looking Back on the Vietnam War* (pp. 79-94). Westport, CT: Greenwood Press.

Herring, G. C. (1993b). The Reluctant Warrior: Lyndon Johnson as Commander I n Chief. In F. L. Anderson (Ed.), *Shadow on the White House: Presidents and the Vietnam War* (pp. 87-112). Lawrence, KA: University of Kansas Press

Herring, G. C. (1994). *LBJ and Vietnam: A Different Kind of War.* Austin, TX: University of Texas Press.

Herring, G. C., and Immerman, R. H. (1984). Eisenhower, Dulles, and Dien Bien Phu: The Day We Didn't Go To War Revisited. *Journal of American History, 71,* 343-363.

Herrman, C. F. (1993). Avoiding Pathologies in Foreign Policy Decision Groups. In D. Caldwell and T. J. McKeown (Eds.), *Diplomacy, Force, and Leadership: Essays in Honor of Alexander L. George* (pp. 179-208). Boulder, CO: Westview Press.

Hess, G. R. (1998). *Vietnam and the United States: Origins and Legacy of War.* (Rev. ed.). New York: Twayne Publishers.

Hilsman, R. (1967). *To Move a Nation: The Politics of Foreign Policy in the Administration of John F. Kennedy.* Garden City, NY: Doubleday.

Hixon, L. W. (2000). *The United States and the Vietnam War: Significant Scholarly Articles.* New York: Garland Publishing, Inc.

Hogwood, B. W., and Peters, G. (1985). *Pathology of Public Policy.* New York: Oxford University Press.

Hood, D. E. (1982). *Lessons of the Vietnam War: Henry Kissinger, George Kennan, Richard Falk and the Debate over Containment, 1965-1980.* Seattle, WA: University of Washington.

Hoopes, T. (1969). *The Limits of Intervention.* New York: David McKay and Company.

Houghton, D. P. (1998). Analogical Reasoning and Policymaking: Where and When is it Used? *Policy Sciences, 31,* 151-176.

Hunt, M. (1996). *Crises in U. S. Foreign Policy.* New Haven, CT: Yale University Press.

Hunt, R. A., and Schutz, R. A., Jr. (Eds.). (1982). *Lessons from an Unconventional War: Reassessing U.S. Strategies for Future Conflict.* New York: Pergamon Press.

Hybel, A. (1991). Learning and Reasoning by Analogy. In M. Fry (Ed.), *History, the White House and the Kremlin: Statesman as Historians.* New York: Pinter Publishers.

Isaacs, A. R. (1997). *Vietnam Shadows: The War, Its Ghosts, and Its Legacy.* Baltimore, MD: Johns Hopkins University Press.

Janis, I. L. (1989). *Crucial Decisions: Leadership in Policymaking and Crisis Management.* New York: Free Press.

Janis, I. L., and Mann, L. (1977). *Decisionmaking: A Psychological Analysis of Conflict, Choice, and Commitment.* New York: Free Press.

Janis, I., and Mann, L. (1992). Cognitive Complexity in International Decisionmaking. In P. Suedfeld and P. E. Tetlock. *Psychology and Social Policy* (pp. 33-49). New York: Hemisphere Publishing Corporation.

Jarosz, W. W. (1993). The Shadow of the Past: Learning from History in National Security Decision Making. In P. E. Tetlock, , J. L. Husbands, R. Jervis, P. C. Stern, C. Tilly. (Eds.). *Behavior, Society, and International Conflict* (vol 3, pp. 126-189). New York: Oxford University Press.

Jentleson, B. W. (Ed.). (2000). *Opportunities Missed, Opportunities Seized: Preventive Diplomacy in the Post-Cold War World.* New York: Rowman & Littlefield Publishers, Inc.

Jervis, R. (1970). *The Logic of Images in International Relations.* Princeton, NJ: Princeton University Press.

Jervis, R. (1997). *System Effects: Complexity in Political and Social Life.* Princeton, NJ: Princeton University Press.

Kahneman, D., and Tversky, A. (1979). Prospect Theory: An Analysis of Decision Under Risk. *Econometrica, 47,* 263-291.

Kahneman, D., and Tversky, A. (1984). Choices, Values, and Frames. *American Psychologist, 39*(4), 341-350.

Kahneman, D., and Tversky, A. (Eds). (2000). *Choices, Values, and Frames.* New York: Cambridge University Press.

Kahin, G. M., and Lewis, J. L. (1967). *The United States in Vietnam.* New York: Dial Press.

Karnow, S. (1983). *Vietnam: A History*. New York: Viking Press.

Katsiaficas, G. (Ed.). (1992). *Vietnam Documents: American and Vietnamese Views of the War*. Armonk, NY: M. E. Sharpe, Inc.

Kattenburg, P. M. (1980). *The Vietnam Trauma in American Foreign Policy*. New Brunswick, NJ: Transactions Publishers.

Kattenburg, P. M. (1987). Reflections on Vietnam: Of Revisionism and Lessons Yet to be Learned. In L. J. Matthews and D. E. Brown (Eds), *Assessing the Vietnam War: A Collection from the Journal of the U.S. Army War College* (pp. 159-170). Washington, DC: Pergamon-Brassey's.

Kattenburg, P. M. (2000). Vietnam and U.S. Diplomacy. In L. W. Hixon (Ed.), *Leadership and Diplomacy in the Vietnam War* (pp. 148-172). New York: Garland Publishing.

Keane, M. T. (1988). *Analogical Problem Solving*. Chichester, UK: Ellis Horwood.

Kenney, S. F. (1978). *Vietnam Decision-Making: A Psychological Perspective on American Foreign Policy*. Boston, MA: Boston University Graduate School.

Kharbanda, O. P., and Stallworthy. E. A. (1984). *How to Learn from Project Disasters*: *True Life Stories with a Moral for Management*. Aldershott, UK: Gower.

Khong, Y. F. (1992a). *Analogies at War: Korea, Munich, Dien Bien Phu and the Vietnam Decision*. Princeton, NJ: Princeton University Press.

Khong, Y. F. (1992b). Vietnam, the Gulf, and U.S. Choices: A Comparison. *Security Studies, 2*, 74-95.

Kimball, J. (1990). *To Reason Why: The Debate abut the Causes of US Involvement in Vietnam*. New York: McGraw-Hill.

Kinnard, D. (1977). *The War Managers*. Hanover, NH: University Press of New England.

Kissinger, H. (1969). The Viet Nam Negotiations. *Foreign Affairs, 47*, 211-234.

Kleinman, F. K. (1980). The Lost Lesson of Vietnam. *Military Review, 60* (9), 64-71.

Kolko, G. (1985). *Anatomy of a War: Vietnam, the United States, and the Modern Historical Experience* (1st ed). New York: Pantheon Books.

Komer, R. W. (1972). *Bureaucracy Does Its Thing: Institutional Constraints on U.S.-GVN Performance in Vietnam*. Santa Monica, CA: Rand Corporation.

Kotler, M. (1965, June-July). Notes on the Vietnam War. *Liberation,* X (4), 12-15.

Kramer, R. (1998). Revisiting the Bay of Pigs and Vietnam Decisions 25 years later: How Well Had the Groupthink Hypothesis Stood the Test of Time. *Organization and Decision Sciences, 73* (2/3), 236-269.

Kraslow, D., and Loory, S. H. (1968). *The Secret Search for Peace in Vietnam*. New York: Random House.

Kuhn, T. S. (1970). *The Structure of Scientific Revolutions* (2nd ed. enl.). Chicago, IL: University of Chicago Press.

Lamb, C. J. (1989). *Belief Systems and Decision Making in the Mayaguez Crisis*. Gainesville, FL: University of Florida Press.

Langguth, A. J. (2000). *Our Vietnam: The War 1954-1975*. New York: Simon and Schuster.

Lebow, N. R., and Stein, J. G. (1996). Back to the Past: Counterfactuals and the Cuban Missile crisis. In P. E. Tetlock and A. Belkin (Eds.), *Counterfactual Thought Experiments in World Politics: Logical, Methodological, and Psychological Perspectives* (pp. 119-148). Princeton, NJ: Princeton University Press.

Leng, R. *Interstate Crisis Behavior, 1816-1980: Problems in Reciprocity*. Cambridge, UK: Cambridge University Press.

Lens, S. (1966, January). Vietnam: A Policy of Deceit. *The Progressive,* 117.

Levy, D. W. (1991). *The Debate over Vietnam*. Baltimore, MD: Johns Hopkins University Press.

Levy, J. S. (1994). Learning and Foreign Policy: Sweeping a Conceptual Minefield. *International Organization, 48,* 279-312.

Levy, J. S. (1997). Prospect Theory, Rational Choice, and International Relations. *International Studies Quarterly, 41,* 87-112

Levy, J. S. (1998). Loss Aversion, Framing, and Bargaining: The Implications of Prospect Theory for International Conflict. In F. P. Harvey and B. D. Mor (Eds.), *Conflicts in World Politics: Advances in the Study of Crisis, War, and Peace* (pp. 96-115). New York: St. Martin's Press.

Lewis, D. K. (1973). *Counterfactuals*. Cambridge, MA: Harvard University Press.

Lind, M. (2000). *Vietnam: The Necessary War*. New York: The Free Press.

Lippman, W. (1959). *The Communist World and Ourselves*. Boston, MA: Little Brown.

Liska, G. (1968). *War and Order: Reflections on Vietnam and History*. Baltimore, MD: Johns Hopkins University Press.

Logevall, F. (1999). *Choosing War: The Lost Chance for Peace and the Escalation of War in Vietnam*. Berkeley, CA: University of California Press.

Lomperis, T. J. (1996). *From People's War to People's Rule*. Chapel Hill, NC: University of North Carolina Press.

MacDonald, D. (1965). Statement on Vietnam. *Partisan Review, 33,* 635-638.

Macdonald, P. G. (1992). *Giap: The Victor in Vietnam*. New York: W. W. Norton & Company.

Maclear, M. (1981). *The Ten Thousand Day War : Vietnam, 1945-1975*. New York : St. Martin's Press.

Mailer, N. (1967). *Why Are We in Vietnam*. New York: Dell.

March, J. G. (1994). *A Primer on Decision Making: How Decisions Happen*. New York: Free Press.

March, J. G. (1997). Understanding How Decisions Happen in Organizations. In Z. Shapira (Ed.). *Organizational Decision Making* (pp. 9-32). New York: Cambridge University Press.

March, J. G., Sproull, L. G., and Tamuz, M. (1996). Learning from Samples of One or Fewer. In M. D. Cohen and L. S. Sproull (Eds.). *Organizational Learning* (pp. 1-19). Thousand Oaks, CA: Sage Publications.

Martino, J. P. (1996). Vietnam and Desert Storm: Learning the Right Lessons from Vietnam for the Post-Cold War Era. Retrieved from Web site www.vietnam.ttu.vietnamcenter/96papers/papers/htm.

May, P. (1992). Policy Learning and Failure. *Journal of Public Policy, 12,* 331-354.

McDermott, R. (1998). *Risk-Taking in International Politics: Prospect Theory in American Foreign Policy*. Ann Arbor, MI: University of Michigan Press.

McMaster, H. R. (1997). *Dereliction of Duty: Lyndon Johnson, Robert McNamara, the Joint Chiefs and the Lies that led to Vietnam*. New York: Harper Collins Publishers.

McNamara, R. S. (1967). *Hearings Before the Committee on Armed Services, Fiscal Year 1967 Supplemental Authorization for Southeast Asia.* Washington, DC: USGPO.

McNamara, R. S. (1969). *Authorization for Military Procurement, Research, and Development, Fiscal Year 1969, and Reserve Strength, Hearings before the Committee on Armed Services, U.S. Senate.* Washington: USGPO.

McNamara, R. S. (1995). *In Retrospect: The Tragedy and Lessons of Vietnam.* New York: Times Books.

McNamara, R. S., Blight, J. G., and Brigham, R. K. (1999). *Argument Without End: In Search of Answers to the Vietnam Tragedy.* New York: Public Affairs.

Menzel, P. T. (Ed.). (1971). *Moral Argument about the War in Vietnam: A Collection of Essays.* Nashville, TN: Aurora.

Milgrom, P. R., and Roberts, J. M. (1986). Relying on the Information of Interested Parties. *Rand Journal of Economics, 17,* 18-32.

Millis, W. (1962). A Liberal Military Defense Policy. In J. Roosevelt (Ed.), *The Liberal Papers* (pp. 97-120). Garden City, NY: Doubleday.

Morgenthau, H. J. (1965, May 1). Russia, the U.S. and Vietnam. *The New Republic,* 12-13.

Mueller, J. E. (1989). The Search for the "Breaking Point" in Vietnam: The Statistics of a Deadly Quarrel. In B. Russett, H. Starr, and R. J. Stoll, (Eds.), *Choices in World Politics: Sovereignty and Interdependence* (pp. 76-93). New York: W. H. Freeman and Company.

Neustadt, R. E., and May, E. R. (1986). *Thinking in Time: The Uses of History for Decision Makers.* New York: The Free Press

Nichols, R. F. (1963). The Genealogy of Historical Generalizations. In L. Gottschalk, (Ed.). *Generalization in the Writing of History* (pp. 130-144). Chicago, IL: University of Chicago Press.

Olson, J. S. (1993). *The Vietnam War: Handbook of the Literature and Research.* Westport, CT: Greenwood Press.

Olson, J. S., and Roberts, R. (1991). *Where the Domino Fell: America and Vietnam, 1945 to 1990.* New York: St. Martin's Press..

O'Neill, B. (1999). *Honors, Symbols, and War.* Ann Arbor, MI: University of Michigan Press.

Organski, A. F. K., and Kugler, J. (1980). *The War Ledger.* Chicago, IL: University of Chicago Press.

Osgood, R. E. (1957). *Limited War: The Challenge to American Strategy.* Chicago, IL: University of Chicago Press.

Osgood, R. E. (1979). *Limited War Revisited.* Boulder, CO: Westview Press.

Palmer, B., Jr. (1984). *The Twenty-five Year War: America's Military Role in Vietnam.* Lexington, KY: University Press of Kentucky.

Patton, C. V., and Sawicki, D. S. (1986). *Basic Methods of Policy Analysis and Planning.* Englewood Cliffs, NJ: Prentice Hall.

Pearlman, M. D. (1999). *Warmaking and American Democracy: The Struggle over Military Strategy, 1700 to the Present.* Lawrence, KA: University Press of Kansas.

The Pentagon Papers: The Defense Department History of United States Decision-making on Vietnam. The Senator Gravel Edition (5 vols.). Boston: Beacon Press.

Peterson, R., Owens, P. D., Tetlock, P. E., Fan, E. T., and Martorana, P. (1998). Group Dynamics in Top Management Teams: Groupthink, Vigilance, and Alternative Models of Organizational Failure. *Organizational Behavior and Human Decision Processes, 73*(2/3), 272-305.

Petraeus, D. H. (1987). Lessons of History and Lessons of Vietnam. In L. J. Matthews and D. E. Brown, (Eds.). *Assessing the Vietnam War: A Collection from the Journal of the U.S. Army War College* (pp. 171-185). Washington, DC: Pergamon-Brassey's.

Pfeffer, R. M. (Ed.). (1968). *No More Vietnams: The War and the Future of American Foreign Policy.* New York: Harper & Row, Publishers.

Podhoretz, N. (1982). *Why We Were in Vietnam.* New York: Simon and Schuster.

Ponder, D. E. (2000). *Good Advice: Information & Policy Making in the White House.* College Station, TX: Texas A&M University Press.

Prados, J. (1995). *The Hidden History of the Vietnam War.* Chicago, IL: Ivan R. Dee.

Raskin, M. G., and Fall, B. B. (1967). *The Viet-Nam Reader: Articles and Documents on American Foreign Policy and the Viet-Nam Crisis.* New York: Vintage Books.

Ravenal, E. (1978). *Never Again: Learning from America's Foreign Policy Failures.* Philadelphia, PA: Temple University Press.

Record, J. (1998). *The Wrong War: Why We Lost in Vietnam.* Annapolis, MD: Naval Institute Press.

Ridgeway, M. B., Gen. (1967). On Vietnam. In M. G. Raskin and B. B. Fall (Eds.), *The Viet-Nam Reader: Articles and Documents on American Foreign Policy and the Viet-Nam Crisis* (Rev. ed.) (pp. 434-443). New York: Vintage Books.

Robinson, J. P. and Jacobson, S. G. (1969). American Public Opinion about Vietnam. In W. Isard, Vietnam: Some Basic Issues and Alternatives (pp. 63-79). Cambridge, MA: Schenkman Publishing Company.

Roosevelt, J. (Ed.). (1962). *The Liberal Papers*. Garden City, NY: Doubleday.

Rose, R. (1991). What is Lesson-Drawing. *Journal of Public Policy*, *11*, 3-30.

Rose, R. (1993). *Lesson Drawing in Public Policy: A Guide to Learning across Time and Space*. Chatham, NJ: Chatam House.

Rosen, S. P. (1982). Vietnam and the American Theory of Limited war. International Security, *7*(2), 83-113.

Rosenberg, M. J., Verba, S., and Converse, P. E. (1970). *Vietnam and the Silent Majority: The Dove's Guide*. New York: Harper and Row.

Rostow, W. W. (1996-1997, Winter). The Case for the Vietnam War. *Parameters: US Army War College Quarterly*, *XXVI* (4), 39-50.

Royal United Services Institute. (1969). *Lessons from the Vietnam War*. London: Royal United Services Institute.

Russo, J. E., and Schoemaker, P. J. H. (1989). *Decision Traps: Ten Barriers to Brilliant Decision-Making and How to Overcome Them*. New York: Doubleday/Currency.

Sacramento State College. (1970). *Viet Nam Bibliography* (Rev. ed). Sacramento, CA: Sacramento State College.

Salisbury, H. (Ed.). (1984). *Vietnam Reconsidered: Lessons from a War*. New York: Harper and Row.

Samuelson, P. A. (1964). *Economics: An Introductory Analysis* (6th ed.). New York: McGraw Hill.

Sanders, S. W., and Henderson, W. (1977). The Consequences of Vietnam. *Orbis*, *21*, 61-76.

Schelling, T. C. (1960). *The Strategy of Conflict*. Cambridge, MA: Harvard University Press.

Schlesinger, A. (1965). *A Thousand Days: John F. Kennedy in the White House*. Boston, MA: Houghton Miflin Company.

Schlesinger, A. (1967). *The Bitter Heritage: Vietnam and American Democracy, 1941-1966.* Greenwich, CT: Fawcett.

Schön, D., and Rein, M. (1994). *Frame Reflection: Toward the Resolution of Intractable Policy Controversies.* New York: Basic Books.

Schwenk, C. R. (1996). Information, Cognitive Biases, and Commitment to a Course of Action. *Academy of Management Review, 11,* 298-310.

Senge, P. M. (1990). *The Fifth Discipline: The Art and Practice of the Learning Organization.* New York: Doubleday.

Senge, P. M. et al. (1999). *The Dance of Change: The Challenges of Sustaining Momentum in Learning Organizations.* New York: Currency/Doubleday.

Shapira, Z. (Ed.). (1997). *Organizational Decision Making.* New York: Cambridge University Press.

Shaplen, R. (1971). *The Road from War: Vietnam 1965-1971.* New York: Harper & Row.

Sharp, U. S. G., Adm. (1967). Testimony. In United States. Congress. Senate. Committee on Armed Services. Preparedness Investigating Subcommittee, *Air War against North Vietnam.* Washington: DC: USGPO.

Slater, J. (1987). Dominos in Central America: Will they Fall? Does it Matter? *International Security, 12 (2),* 105-134.

Small, M. (1988). *Johnson, Nixon, and the Doves.* New Brunswick, NJ: Rutgers University Press.

Smith, R. B. (1983). *An International History of the Vietnam War.* London: St. Martin's Press.

Sorensen, T. (1971). *Kennedy.* New York: Harper and Row.

Sorley, L. (1999). *A Better War: The Unexamined Victories and Final Tragedy of America's Last Years in Vietnam.* New York: Harcourt Brace and Company

Stam, A. C., III (1996). *Win, Lose, or Draw: Domestic Politics and the Crucible of War.* Ann Arbor, MI: University of Michigan Press.

Stanton, S. (1985). *The Rise and Fall of an American Army: U.S. Ground Forces in Vietnam, 1965-1973.* New York: Dell.

Staw, B. M. (1976). Knee Deep in the Big Muddy: A Study of Escalation Commitment to a Chosen Course of Action. *Organizational Behavior and Human Performance, 16,* 27-44.

Staw. B. M., and Fox, F. (1977). Escalation: Some Determinants of Commitment to a Previously Chosen Course of Action. *Human Relations, 30,* 431-450.

Staw, B. M. and Ross, J. (1989). Understanding Behavior in Escalation Situations. *Science, 246,* 216-220.

Steinberg, B. S. (1996). *Shame and Humiliation: Presidential Decision Making on Vietnam.* Pittsburgh, PA: University of Pittsburgh Press.

Suedfeld, P., and Tetlock, P. E. (1992). Psychological Advice about Political Decisionmaking: Heuristics, Biases, and Cognitive Defects. In P. S. Suedfeld and P. E. Tetlock (Eds.), *Psychology and Social Policy* (pp. 51-70). New York: Hemisphere Publishing Company.

Summers, H. G. (1982). *On Strategy: A Critical Analysis of the Vietnam War.* Novato, CA: Presidio Press.

Sylvan, D., and Majeski, S. (1998). A Methodology for the Study of Historical Counterfactuals. *Organizational Studies Quarterly, 42,* 79-108.

Taylor, M., Gen. (1966). Testimony. In United States Congress. Senate Committee on Foreign Relations. *The Vietnam Hearings.* New York: Vintage Books.

Tetlock, P. E., and Mor, C., Jr. (1986). Cognitive Aspects in Foreign Policy. In R. K. White (Ed.), *Psychology and the Prevention of Nuclear War: A Book of Readings* (pp. 147-179). New York: New York University Press.

Tetlock, P. E., and Belkin, A. (1996). Counterfactual Thought Experiments in World Politics: Logical, Methodological, and Psychological Perspectives. In P. E. Tetlock and A. Belkin (Eds.), *Counterfactual Thought Experiments in World Politics* (pp. 1-38). Princeton, NJ: Princeton University Press.

't Hart, P. (1994). *Group Think in Government.* Baltimore, MD: The Johns Hopkins University Press.

Thompson, W. S. and Frizzell, D. D. (1977). *The Lessons of Vietnam*. New York: Crane, Russak and Company, Incorporated

Thomson, D. (1967). The Writing of Contemporary History. *Journal of Contemporary History, 2,* 25-34.

Tilford, E. H. (1991). *Setup: What the Air Force Did in Vietnam and Why.* Maxwell AFB, AL: Air University Press.

Tomes, R. R. (1998). *Apocalypse Then: American Intellectuals and the Vietnam War, 1954-1975.* New York: New York University Press.

Tucker, S. C. (1998). *Encyclopedia of the Vietnam War: A Political, Social, and Military History* (3 vols). Santa Barbara, CA: ABC-Clio.

Tversky, A. and Kahneman, D. (1986). Rational Choice and the Framing of Decisions. *Journal of Business, 59,* S251-S278.

U.S. Congress. House Committee on Armed Services. (1967a). *Fiscal Year 1967 Supplemental Authorization of Southeast Asia .* Washington, DC: USGPO.

U.S. Congress. Senate Committee on Armed Services. Preparedness Investigating Subcommittee. (1967b). *Air War Against North Vietnam.* Washington, DC: USGPO

U.S. Government. (1985). *United States Forces in Vietnam, 1965-1973.* New York: Dell.

Van De Mark, B. (1991). *Into the Quagmire: Lyndon Johnson and the Escalation of the Vietnam War.* New York: Oxford University Press.

Vandiver, F. E. (1997). *Shadows of Vietnam: Lyndon Johnson's Wars.* College Station, TX: Texas A&M University Press.

Van Evera, S. (1990, July). The Case Against Intervention. *Atlantic, 266,* 72-80.

Vertzberger, Y. (1990). *The World in Their Minds: Information Processing, Cognition, and Perception in Foreign Policy Decision Making.* Stanford, CA: Stanford University Press.

Voss, J. F. and Dorsey, J. D. (1990). Perception and International Relations: An Overview. In E. Singer and V. Hudson

(Eds.). *Political Psychology and Foreign Policy* (pp. 13-30). Boulder, CO: Westview Press.

Warburg, J. (1962). A Re-Examination of American Foreign Policy. In J. Roosevelt (Ed.), *The Liberal Papers* (pp. 49-96). Garden City, NY: Doubleday.

Webb, E. J. (1968). A Review of Social Science Research in Vietnam with Procedural Recommendations for Future Research in Insurgent Settings. Arlington, VA: Institute for Defense Analysis.

Weimer, D. L., and Quinn, A. (1992). *Policy Analysis: Concepts and Practices* (2nd Ed.). Englewood Cliffs, NJ: Prentice Hall.

Werner, J. S., and Huhyn, K. L. (Eds.). (1993). *The Vietnam War: Vietnamese and American Perspectives*. Armonk, NY: M. E. Sharpe.

Westmoreland, W. G., Gen. (1968). Report on the Operation in South Vietnam. In U.S. Pacific Command, *Report on the War in Vietnam*, Section II. Washington, DC: USGPO.

Westmoreland, W. G., Gen. (1976). *A Soldier Reports*. New York: Garden City, NY: Doubleday.

Westmoreland, W. G., Gen. (1979). Vietnam in Perspective. *Military Review, 59*, 34-63.

Wheeler, E., Gen. (1967). Testimony. In United States. Congress. Senate. Committee on Armed Services. Preparedness Investigating Subcommittee, *Air War against North Vietnam*. Washington: DC: USGPO.

Whitworth, W. (1970). *Naive Questions about War and Peace*. New York: W. W. Norton.

Wicker, T. (1968). *LBJ: The Influence of Personality upon Politics*. New York: Morrow.

Winters, F. X. (1997). *The Year of the Hare: America in Vietnam, January 25, 1963-February 15, 1964*. Athens, GA: University of Georgia Press.

Wirtz, J. J. (1991). *The Tet Offensive: Intelligence Failure in War*. Ithaca, NY: Cornell University Press.

Young, M. B. (1991). *The Vietnam Wars, 1945-1990*. New York: HarperCollins.

Zaroulis, N., and Sullivan, S. G. (1984*). Who Spoke Up? American Protest against the Vietnam War, 1963-1975.* Garden City, NY: Doubleday.

Zinn, H. (1967). *Vietnam: The Logic of Withdrawal.* Boston, MA: Beacon Press.

Zumwalt, E. (1997). Preface. In S. Tucker, *Encyclopedia of the Vietnam War* (pp. ixx-xx). Santa Barbara, CA: ABC-Clio.

INDEX

A

air interdiction, 75, 83, 85
Alsop, Joseph, 15
analogies, 23, 30, 102, 133, 141
anti-domino theory, 98
ARVN (Army of the Republic of Vietnam), 60, 72, 76, 80, 81
attrition strategy, 59, 69, 136

B

Ball, George, 27n10, 47n42, 135
body count, 81, 136n5
bombing halt, 91-92
bombing of North Vietnam, 11, 52, 59, 75, 77, 113
   closing land and sea routes, 88
   escalation, 90
   signal content, 68
   U.S. strategy, 84
Bundy, McGeorge, 2n3, 49-50
Bundy, William P., 35, 44
"butterfly" effects, 145

C

Carter, Jimmy, 151
Chamberlain, Neville, 133
checklists for decisionmaking, 139-142
China, 22, 74, 97, 99, 131
Chomsky, Noam, 2, 125
CIA (Central Intelligence Agency), 51
civilian decisionmakers' model, 18-22
Clifford, Clark, 82-83, 92
Clinton, William J., ix
Cohen, William, ix
cold war, 18, 32, 97, 110, 113, 114, 138, 141, 147
counterfactual policy models, 147
   advocacy and values, 147
   historical tests for, 143-144
   statistical inference in, 143
counterfactual propositions, 15
counterinsurgency, 28
   force ratios required for successful, 39